LET MY PEOPLE KNOW

THE INCREDIBLE STORY
OF **MIDDLE EAST PEACE** —
AND **WHAT LIES AHEAD**

ARYEH LIGHTSTONE

Encounter
BOOKS

New York • London

First American edition published in 2022 by Encounter Books,
an activity of Encounter for Culture and Education, Inc.,
a nonprofit, tax-exempt corporation.
Encounter Books website address: www.encounterbooks.com

Manufactured in the United States and printed on
acid-free paper. The paper used in this publication meets
the minimum requirements of ANSI/NISO Z39.48–1992
(R 1997) (*Permanence of Paper*).

FIRST AMERICAN EDITION

LIBRARY OF CONGRESS CATALOGING-IN-PUBLICATION DATA

Names: Lightstone, Aryeh, 1980– author.
Title: Let my people know : the incredible story of Middle East peace—
and what lies ahead / Aryeh Lightstone.
Description: First American edition. | New York, New York : Encounter Books, 2022.
Includes bibliographical references and index.
Identifiers: LCCN 2021052375 (print) | LCCN 2021052376 (ebook)
ISBN 9781641772648 (hardcover) | ISBN 9781641772655 (ebook)
Subjects: LCSH: Lightstone, Aryeh, 1980– | Friedman, David Melech.
Arab-Israeli conflict—1993—Peace. | Diplomats—United
States—Biography. | Israel—Foreign relations—Islamic countries.
Islamic countries—Foreign relations—Israel. | United States—Foreign
relations—2017–2021. | United States—Foreign relations—Israel.
Israel—Foreign relations—United States.
Classification: LCC DS119.76 .L54 2022 (print) | LCC DS119.76 (ebook)
DDC 956.05/3—dc23/eng/20211209
LC record available at https://lccn.loc.gov/2021052375
LC ebook record available at https://lccn.loc.gov/2021052376

1 2 3 4 5 6 7 8 9 20 22

CONTENTS

INTRODUCTION

For four years, I had the honor of representing the United States of America first as the senior advisor to the U.S. ambassador to Israel, David Friedman, and then as the special envoy for economic normalization for the Abraham Accords. I was an ordinary person blessed with an extraordinary opportunity and the chance to witness history as it was being made. During those years, I frequently sat in the room with others who likewise thought of themselves as ordinary people set in positions of extraordinary importance—particularly Ambassador Friedman, but also many others such as Jared Kushner, Mike Pompeo, and Nikki Haley, to name just a few. They took their jobs extremely seriously and treasured each moment they had to make a difference. I learned invaluable lessons from my boss and my colleagues, and from leaders I interacted with in Israel and the Abraham Accords countries.

This book was written to let my people know what I saw and learned, and to share my thoughts about how the United States can build upon the unprecedented success of the Trump administration's Middle East policy culminating in the historic Abraham Accords. Middle East peace had always been regarded as an unsolvable puzzle. Here I explain the principles that were applied to prepare the way for solving it. I bring readers into the room with me to watch as policies are being formulated.

Where I use quotation marks, readers should understand that I am generally giving a close approximation of the words spoken. There are personal vignettes, but no damaging revelations about anyone. With very few exceptions, the people I worked with were admirable and did their very best to advance the interests of the United States.

Because I am writing from my direct experience, I devote considerable space to my own activities on the job. It is first of all my personal story. But I always understood that my experience was part of a much bigger story. I can illustrate the point with a story that I read when I was ten years old and recounted many times to groups I met with in Israel. Right after the basketball game in 1962 where Wilt Chamberlain famously scored 100 points, a reporter asked a team member who had scored 2 points how the game would be remembered in history. Without hesitation he answered, "Tonight will be remembered for all of history as the night that Wilt and I combined to score 102 points." I have since learned that the story is apocryphal, but I am sharing it because in my embassy job I was rather like the anonymous 2-point shooter in Chamberlain's 100-point game.

I was offered the position of senior advisor by David Friedman because he knew me personally, and for the next four years I spent every waking hour trying to repay the trust that he—and through him, the U.S. government—had placed in me. History will credit the courage and vision of some remarkable leaders during those four years, but visionary leaders need team members who can execute their ideas. I am proud to have been part of a great team working on behalf of the greatest country in the history of the world. I want to Let My People Know that history was made in the Middle East during the four years of the Trump administration. This book is intended to showcase the ideas and policies that brought success and to demonstrate how best to build upon it in the future.

I

"I HAVE MY CANDIDATE"

The U.S. Embassy in Israel never had a true political appointee, from outside the professional foreign policy world, before President Trump nominated David Friedman to serve as his ambassador to Israel. That nomination was a shock to the system. Friedman was not a known personality in Washington, D.C., but his writings and charitable involvement left no doubt that he would be unapologetically pro-Israel. It was even more of a shock when I was appointed as his senior advisor.

There are fewer than ten politically appointed special advisors posted to our embassies around the world at any point in time. It takes substantial resources to train, house, and secure American personnel abroad. In the case of career foreign service professionals, this is a sunk cost, but for political appointees it is an expenditure to be carefully meted out where necessary. Political appointments are normally reserved for the highest-profile and busiest posts abroad. For the U.S. Embassy in Israel to receive two political appointees before ambassadors had been nominated to most of our major allies was unprecedented. These appointments signaled that there was going to be a new direction in Middle East policy. In fact, my embassy job would give me an inside perspective on a breakthrough in the region, culminating in the four Abraham Accords signed between September 15 and December 23, 2020.

The way I came to be appointed gave me a clue about how the soil was being tilled for a realignment of Middle East policy. On February 9, 2017, David and I were on the Accela heading from Washington back to our homes on Long Island after an exhausting day of meetings with members of Congress. Our last meeting had been with Senator Bernie Sanders, and we weren't in great spirits when we boarded the train. As the car rocked back and forth, we talked intermittently about the day's meetings, checked our phones, and dozed a little.

Then David mentioned his meeting with President Trump earlier that day. "The president wants me to work closely with Jared Kushner on the Mideast peace team," he said. "It is a great honor, but I need to bring along a chief of staff I can trust, to assist me as I repair the U.S.-Israel relationship that's been gravely injured over the past eight years. It is rare that ambassadors can hire someone to come with them, so I want to get a commitment from this person quickly."

"Do you have a short list of candidates you want to interview?" I asked. "If so, I could be helpful setting them up."

"I have my candidate. It's you."

David had been a friend and mentor for almost a decade. His wife, Tammy, was one of the very first people to welcome my wife and me to our community on Long Island when we moved there ten years earlier. During the Republican primaries of 2016, David and I had a friendly rivalry, as I favored Marco Rubio while he supported his good friend Donald Trump. After Trump's victory, I was anxious to do everything I could to help David become the ambassador to Israel, and I offered my assistance in the confirmation process. He accepted, and I'm really not sure why, since many of his friends have relationships in the U.S.

Senate similar to mine, and I spent the better part of two months traveling back and forth from Long Island to D.C. with David for his Senate confirmation and State Department onboarding. I was not-so-secretly hoping for an opportunity to work with David at the embassy, but I doubted that there was actually an appropriate position for me. When he offered me a job assisting him, I doubted that I was the right person for it.

"Thank you for this opportunity," I said to David. "It's extremely humbling to be considered." I promised to discuss it with my wife, Estee, and get back to him in a day or two.

It was two days later when I went to David's house with a pit in my stomach. I told him that serving as his advisor could be the best job in the world, but the timing wasn't great for my family. More importantly, I suggested that he find someone better qualified for the position.

"Why aren't you 'qualified'?" he asked.

I explained my thinking: "You and I agree on almost everything. We are unapologetically pro-Israel. We are conservatives. We know the relationship needs to be repaired. And we both saw very clearly the foolishness of the Iran deal and the 'peace' processes." I noted that David had a big challenge ahead of him and that I might only compound the difficulty. "The world already discounts you for being the son of a rabbi and an Orthodox Jew. You will be cementing their worst fears by hiring someone who is an Orthodox rabbi, and someone who wears a kippa at all times. Why don't you hire someone else who agrees with us—there are plenty of others—and ideally, someone who is ..." I hesitated before saying, "not as Jewish."

David thought for a few moments, and then replied with words that echo in my head to this day: "I don't know what job you think you were offered. If you think I offered a job representing the United States of America to the State of Israel in which being a rabbi and an Orthodox Jew is a disqualification, then I offered the position to the wrong person. But if you want a job representing the United States of America being proud of who you are, knowing who you are, supporting what you believe in, that is the job I am offering, and I hope it is the one you will take."

As he spoke, I came to understand three things very distinctly.

First, I had to work for this person. His clarity of thought and purpose was infectious.

Second, being pro-Israel is not a bug in the system of being American. It is a feature of our national character.

Third, if you want to represent the greatest country in history and do it successfully, you'd better start acting the part. That means being bold, clear, and unapologetic, as I knew that David Friedman would be. He demanded the same from his entire team, especially me.

That is how I became an eyewitness to some of America's greatest foreign policy successes in the Middle East, and, I believe, some of the most momentous in all of U.S. history. This book is to let my people, meaning all my fellow Americans, know what exactly were the big ideas that propelled these successes, and that can continue to foster peace in the Middle East and help restore our nation to its position of world leadership.

2

DENIALISM

If it weren't so painfully awkward, it would have been hysterical. In May 2021, Matthew Lee, a seasoned diplomatic correspondent for the Associated Press, asked President Biden's State Department spokesperson, Ned Price, to name the agreements that had recently been signed between Israel and several Middle Eastern countries under his boss's predecessor. In a series of back-and-forth questions, Price twisted himself into a pretzel to avoid naming the Abraham Accords. The cringe-inducing exchange reminded me of what my daughter would do when she was younger and afraid of something that was happening in front of her. She would close her eyes and simply refuse to acknowledge the reality.

The refusal to call the Abraham Accords by their name, and the broader effort to downplay their significance, can be written off to a combination of childishness and petty partisanship. But the more I think about it, the more I am convinced that refusing to look reality in the face has been at the heart of U.S. policy in the Middle East for 68 of the past 72 years.

The denialism perhaps reached its height of delusionality—and dangerousness—during Barack Obama's presidency, in two key policy choices. One was his dogged pursuit of a nuclear deal with Iran, culminating in an agreement that in the best case would allow Iran to have legal nuclear capability within fifteen years, and in the worst case, or as I perceive it the reality, allow it the cash to strengthen its autocratic regime and increase its malign activities throughout the region while giving it the veneer of a legitimate state actor. The second choice was placing the Israeli-Palestinian conflict at the center of Middle East policy, essentially saying it was the root cause of many if not all the challenges plaguing the Middle East, and holding that the wider region cannot move forward until it is resolved in an "evenhanded" way. President Obama's secretary of state during his second term, John Kerry, summed up the administration's policy stance in 2016 when he said, "There will be no separate peace between Israel and the Arab world." In other words, there was no chance of normalization between Israel and Arab countries until the Israeli-Palestinian conflict was resolved in a way that was satisfactory to the Palestinians. For emphasis, Kerry added, "No, no, no," echoing the infamous Three No's that entered the world's political lexicon in 1967.

In the wake of their defeat in the Six-Day War, the Arab League met in Khartoum, the capital of Sudan, and issued a set of resolutions, most notably including: "no peace with Israel, no recognition of Israel, no negotiations with it." This resolution became not only the basis of the Palestinian negotiating strategy, but also a principle affirmed through the decades even by U.S. leadership. The persistent hold of the Three No's explains why the Middle East has been a constant source of challenge for the United States, and why we haven't been able to unlock the boundless possibility of the region.

The words of a diplomat matter a lot, and Kerry, as the United States of America's chief diplomat, chose to reinforce Arab inflexibility on the conditions for progress and peace at the expense of our democratic ally, the State of Israel. If the policy is essentially to take the position of those who do not really want peaceful coexistence, it will not lead to peace. Promoting this wrong-headed policy made the United States weaker in the region and around the world. On the other hand, adopting policies that are better aligned with our values and interests will make us more respected and stronger.

The Three No's have allowed the Palestinians to exercise veto power over progress in the region and even over U.S. policy and law, particularly the Jerusalem Embassy Act, which was passed by an overwhelming bipartisan majority in 1995. This law required the president to recognize Jerusalem as the capital of Israel, move the U.S. Embassy there from Tel Aviv, and establish the residency of the U.S. ambassador to Israel in Jerusalem. According to the Constitution, however, foreign policy is primarily the president's responsibility. So Congress made those provisions a trigger to release certain funds to the State Department, and included a waiver provision whereby the president could choose not to follow the law if it was deemed contrary to national security interests.

After the Jerusalem Embassy Act became law, every major presidential candidate promised to move the U.S. Embassy to Jerusalem. Every six months, year after year—until December 2017—every president signed the waiver and took no steps to fulfill the law. Poll after poll consistently showed that recognizing Jerusalem as Israel's capital and moving the embassy would be widely welcomed. Yet it took twenty-two years for the law to be put into effect because of the de facto Palestinian veto and the refusal to acknowledge Israel as a legitimate state.

3

COVID DIPLOMACY

To the rest of the world, it may have appeared that the Abraham Accords came about suddenly, with one crucial decision. The truth is that the Accords, like every major world event, were the culmination of many smaller, unnoticed developments. One that I saw up close was the willingness of Arab states to lend assistance to Israel during the coronavirus pandemic in 2020.

In the early days of Covid-19, the U.S. State Department carried out one of the biggest repatriation efforts in history. Under the leadership of Mike Pompeo, it facilitated the return of at least a million U.S. citizens in extraordinarily difficult circumstances, bringing Americans home from every country and territory on earth, including some with which we have no diplomatic relations. Israel reached out to us for help in its own repatriation challenge. Israelis travel more than most people, sometimes making it into countries with which their government has no diplomatic relations. In normal times, this should be discouraged. In a pandemic, it could be deadly. The Israeli Prime Minister's Office called my boss, Ambassador Friedman, and asked if we could help repatriate hundreds of Israelis from countries that had less than ideal relations, if any, with Israel, but did have relations with the United States. The ambassador asked me to liaise with Secretary Pompeo's team, and we went to work.

It is not remarkable that we helped Israelis. That is what friends do. What's remarkable is that countries with which Israel had no relations did not hesitate to help when we asked. They removed every piece of red tape to allow Israelis to return home. Prior to every phone call I was prepared for diplomatic battle, but it never happened. The calls were pleasant, even friendly. They did not ask why those Israelis were in the country or how they had gotten there. They simply recognized a government's obligation to take care of its citizens in times of crisis, and acted accordingly. I was amazed, but I shouldn't have been.

The Covid-19 crisis also presented me with a striking example of the Palestinian leadership's denialism and how it is harmful to the Palestinian people. I witnessed the strange episode while in an unmarked military base in the middle of Israel on May 21, during one of my biweekly meetings with Maoz, who worked as the special emissary from the Israeli Prime Minister's Office for relations with countries that Israel did not actually have relations with. Maoz was also a critical interlocutor with the Palestinian Authority and some important individuals in Gaza. He hails from a kibbutz with a population of less than two hundred in southern Israel. "Maoz" means "strength" in Hebrew, though it isn't his real name. Maoz has no identifiable personal information, but many cell phones and a command of many languages. He is not exactly the kind of person I would have spent a lot of time with during my previous career as a youth rabbi, yet we became more than friends. We became brothers.

Maoz and I tried to work in close proximity whenever possible. The more that each of us learned about what the other had been working on, the more confident we were that we could create new opportunities for both of our countries. When the U.S. Embassy went to remote work on account of Covid, I was able to spend time two days a week with Maoz.

He was having an animated phone conversation one day when I went to meet with him in a nondescript library on a secret military base. While Israel spends enormous sums on fighter jets and cyber computing, taxpayers can be assured that funds are not being squandered on this facility: the couches predate the War of Independence (1948), and I didn't see any books published after the mid-1980s. As I browsed the shelves, I could tell that Maoz was in the middle of something more interesting than what I was doing.

It turned out that he was coordinating with the United Arab Emirates on sending aid to the Palestinians in the West Bank to help them deal with the coronavirus. Most of the world was struggling to get enough personal protective equipment, respirators, and therapeutics to cope with the pandemic. Most leaders were thrilled when someone with extra supplies was willing to sell. The UAE, renowned for its aid efforts, was donating an entire planeload of critical relief goods. In the Covid lockdowns, the border between Israel and Jordan was closed, so instead of landing an Etihad (UAE national carrier) plane in Amman and then hauling the supplies west to the Jordan Valley, crossing over the Allenby Bridge into the West Bank and driving on to Ramallah, the plan was to touch down at Ben Gurion Airport in Israel, which would cut the driving distance to Ramallah in half.

That is the context of a conversation that blew my socks off. Maoz was on the phone with a Palestinian Authority interlocutor, coordinating the handoff of those critical supplies, when suddenly his face registered astonishment.

"What happened?" I asked.

Still on the phone, he scribbled on a piece of paper: "They

won't take the supplies because the Etihad plane landed in Israel, not Jordan."

I asked Maoz to put the phone on speaker. I had to hear it for myself. Even though my Arabic-language skills are nonexistent, it was clear from his interlocutor's tone that the Palestinian Authority was in fact refusing the aid. Maoz asked five more times. The answer was "no" five more times.

The entire developing world was scrambling for these precious supplies, yet the Palestinian Authority rejected them out of hand just because the airplane carrying them had landed in Israel. Remember that the PA are regarded as moderates who could be reliable peace partners for Israel, yet they would rather harm their own people than budge in their denialism. The rejection of aid from Arab Muslims during a global pandemic illustrated what Ambassador Friedman knew clearly: the so-called Palestinian leadership could not be part of the solution because it was most of the problem.

This was another piece of the puzzle for the leaders of the Arab world. The Palestinians were stuck waiting for a political solution that was becoming more distant by the year, and their rejection of aid in the midst of a pandemic showed how divorced from reality their expectations were. The dynamic, forward-looking Arab leaders were seeking ways not just to compete but to lead in this century. They could see that good relations with Israel would be an asset to them, while the Palestinians under their recalcitrant leaders were a liability. I had recently seen generous cooperation from Arab countries during our mission to repatriate both Americans and Israelis. I knew that John Kerry was wrong in reciting the "no, no, no" doctrine. There were strong and courageous leaders in the Middle East who wanted the future to look decidedly different from the past, and who realized that working together with Israel was part of the formula for a better future.

4

NO-NONSENSE THINKING

M ost presidents have made Middle East peace a focus of a
second term, when they are no longer bound by electoral
politics and can pressure Israel to make unrealistic compromises,
with eyes on a Nobel Prize and a legacy. This was not what pushed
President Trump to engage in the Middle East in a meaningful
way at the beginning of his first term. For one thing, the Middle
East was on fire. Syria was in the midst of a civil war, with terrible human rights violations happening daily. ISIS was still a
force to be reckoned with, and through social media was inciting
and inspiring "cool" extremism around the globe. Yemen was
in tatters. Hezbollah had over 120,000 missiles aimed at Israel.
The Arab Spring, instead of bringing stability to the region, had
stirred up chaos.

The Iran nuclear deal signed in 2015, formally called the Joint
Comprehensive Plan of Action, was looming over the entire
region. Ron Dermer, Israel's ambassador to the United States,
had the most to-the-point description of the existential threat
caused by the deal. He said that in the JCPOA, Iran "was allowed
to do research and development on more and more advanced
centrifuges. So, the nuclear deal with Iran enabled Iran to advance
their nuclear program, under the imprimatur of the international

community—essentially gave a kosher stamp to Iran moving on a path not just on one bomb but to an entire nuclear arsenal."* At its core, the Iran deal was the international community giving the thumbs-up to Iran's nuclear ambitions, not today but in ten years.

It was clear that President Trump had inherited a Middle East in crisis. The question was what an unconventional president would do in a region that was so explosive. The president knew that the United States' Middle East strategy needed rethinking, and that with all of these challenges there was a unique moment in time to strengthen our interests abroad while reducing our risk and exposure. He ran as an unapologetic "America First" candidate, yet he knew that focusing heavily on the Middle East was not a betrayal of his voters. He knew that the United States would need to double down on its principles to have any success in the Middle East, and that these principles would resonate with those who elected him to lead America First. These principles are not complicated:

1. Stand with your allies.
2. Don't yield an inch to adversaries.
3. If you say something, mean something.

The United States would lead with clarity and strength, and it would stop allowing outside players to have a veto over U.S. policy. If we do not respect ourselves on the world stage, we cannot expect the world to respect us. And when we are perceived as weak and indecisive, we are likely to weaken ourselves and our values.

Consider the apologetic approach of Barack Obama, as heralded in his first major speech as president. In the Major Reception Hall at Cairo University, President Obama apologized for

---

* Dmitry Shapiro, "Iran nuclear deal has 'put us on cruise control heading over a cliff,' former envoy says," *Cleveland Jewish News*, December 24, 2021.

previous American actions in the Middle East. What this meant for diplomacy was that there would be little clarity about the United States' intentions in the region or its larger vision for world affairs. But the main takeaway was that America was going to become more internationally inclined. We didn't want to alienate other nations or hurt their feelings. Others described this doctrine as leading from behind, but that isn't leading. It's a fancy way of saying that we will allow others to have an outsized say in the future of our country. The United States would lead under President Obama but as the convenor of experts from various nations to achieve consensus.

President Obama also announced that there would be daylight between the United States and Israel. At first blush, that sounds reasonable. America's government should look out for American interests first and foremost. In theory, there should be daylight between us and every other nation, allowing us to make independent decisions in a fluid and effective way. That's fine in an academic sense, but it can be deadly in the Middle East, because it creates a perception of vulnerability for our chief ally in the region, and perception leads to reality there.

The United States is Israel's greatest asset in projecting strength in the region, so when this alliance appears to be weakened, it will be tested by nefarious actors, of which there is no shortage in the Middle East. If the United States fails the test of standing with our ally, as it did several times under President Obama, then Israel actually becomes weaker in the region, and that is detrimental to U.S. interests as well. Instead of standing unapologetically with our longtime ally, Obama's policy in the region was consistently pushing Israel down to achieve equity with the Palestinians, who are seen as the underdogs. One example of this policy was condemning Israeli home building in the West Bank in the same breath as condemning Palestinian terrorism. Another demonstration of the equity principle was elevating the Palestinian mission in Washington to the diplomatic equivalent of an embassy.

The concept of "equity" as distinct from "equality" has become popular recently, but it has actually been an undercurrent of U.S. foreign policy for decades. Instead of making equal opportunity the operative principle, equity calls for achieving equal outcomes by giving an extra boost to some while putting restraints on others. In this philosophy, it isn't fair that Israel is more successful, so it must be pulled down or held to impossible expectations, while the less successful Palestinians are indulged with double standards.

The equity principle was also revealed in a story that I heard from Mitt Romney when he was a presidential candidate. He recounted the time in 2010 when President Obama called fifty major CEOs to the White House and criticized them for not growing their companies and hiring, even though they had money on the books. Why weren't they spreading the wealth around? Romney explained that the Obama administration had no practical understanding of real-world economics. Companies don't grow and hire simply because they have cash on their balance sheets, but because they understand the regulatory environment and see a path forward. In the equality-of-opportunity philosophy, leadership will do everything in its power to give businesses confidence in their future and clarity about their opportunities, then get out of the way so they can innovate and grow. The philosophy of equity, on the other hand, demands that outcomes be more equalized, even if economics cannot support those outcomes. Obama's uninformed policies led to the slowest economic recovery in modern American history by virtually every measure.

The principle of equity might sound nice from a moral standpoint, but it demands results that don't comport with reality.

Substituting the reality-based idea of equal opportunity with the ideological concept of equity in outcomes causes harm in both domestic and foreign policy. Equity suggests that all nations should be mediocre together, and none should lead. This results in equivocation and weakness where conviction and decisiveness are needed.

What first led me into politics was the JCPOA, the Iran nuclear deal brokered by the Obama administration in 2015. I still do not understand how America could have entered into such a terrible deal—terrible for our own nation and for our allies. The threat of a nuclear-armed Iran to the world and especially to Israel is terrifying. Ambassador Friedman often remarked that while it was possible, at least in theory, that the Iranians would have moderated their behavior when the deal became operative, the cat was out of the bag. In April 2018, on primetime TV, Prime Minister Netanyahu disclosed Iranian documents taken in a daring Mossad operation and explained how they demonstrated that the Iranians never came clean about their nuclear program, as was required in the JCPOA. The documents revealed that the regime would use any and all means to acquire nuclear capabilities and would patiently wait for the JCPOA to run its fifteen-year course. The Iran deal did not address Iran's malign behavior, such as arming terrorist groups throughout the Middle East and beyond, and building a ballistic missile program. The regime continued to show malicious intent by expanding its funding for Hezbollah and the Houthis, and brazenly testing ballistic missiles even while at the negotiating table. The only thing more inexplicable than entering the ill-considered Iran deal would be reentering it.

The inconsistency of U.S. policy on the issue of the Iran deal causes daily confusion in the Middle East and surrounding areas. Like any other part of the world, the Middle East needs order and consistency of expectations. The inability of the United States to be unequivocal in word and deed to stop the Islamic Republic of Iran from gaining nuclear capabilities is one of the biggest causes of strife and mayhem in the Middle East. From Bush to Obama to Trump to Biden, the United States has changed its policy toward Iran. This flipflopping has prompted countries in the region to keep reevaluating and reshuffling their own alliances.

In many speeches and interviews, Ambassador Friedman said, "In the Middle East, you have two choices: You can be strong, or you can be dead." It is an unfortunate reality of the neighborhood. Lack of strength and conviction leads to a power vacuum, which in the Middle East results in confusion, chaos, and terror. A power vacuum is what allowed the growth of an enormous ISIS caliphate, and what continues to permit Iran's terror proxies to cause havoc.

On his first international trip in May 2017, to Saudi Arabia, President Trump warned about the danger of allowing a vacuum to exist. He told the leaders and representatives of the many Arab and Muslim countries attending the summit in Riyadh that it was their responsibility to eliminate Islamic extremism. If they chose not to accept this responsibility, they would continue to bear the brunt of radical Islam, and they would do so alone. He also followed through on his promise to eviscerate the ISIS caliphate, which was completely destroyed by March 23, 2019.

After his visit to Saudi Arabia, President Trump boarded Air Force One and flew to Israel on the first-ever direct flight between the two countries. It's surreal to think that U.S. government officials were previously unable to fly between Israel and many other locations in the region. Countries with which the United States had diplomatic relationships said that our planes had to make "technical stops" in Jordan en route from Israel and also on the way to Israel from their own airports. And our government bowed to those demands for more than seventy years.

What an absolute failure of leadership. The United States is the world's preeminent superpower and the greatest force for good the world has ever seen. When you arrive in any of the countries that imposed those flight restrictions, the people there may or may not like you, but they respect the American flag and what it represents. Yet for several decades the United States played along with unreasonable demands to support the delusion that if you don't acknowledge Israel, it won't exist.

Israelis and Saudis cannot fly to each other's country directly because those countries don't have diplomatic relationships with each other. The United States has a strong relationship with both, and if you were to ask leaders of each country what was its most important ally in the world, the answer would undoubtedly be the United States. We had the leverage to insist on direct flights for U.S. government aircraft, but we didn't use it. Instead, our government had complied with the asinine policy of not recognizing Israel, which sent a message far beyond the countries involved. Every time a plane departed Saudi Arabia and made a "technical stop" in Jordan for an hour or so, the world knew the United States did not stand against the nonrecognition of Israel. The world saw that we didn't even respect ourselves as a nation enough to value our leaders' most valuable commodity, their time.

While certain countries do not yet have official relations with Israel, not a single one of them has a veto on the policies of the United States or a claim on the president's time. That's precisely why President Trump, on his first international trip, flew directly from Saudi Arabia to Israel. The release of Air Force One's flight plan in May 2017 conveyed the first essential message of the Middle East peace agenda: The United States stands with Israel and its other allies. Too often that is a throwaway line, but this direct flight demonstrated it in practice. Beyond that, it showed that the U.S. government was standing resolutely for America itself. The commander in chief and leader of the free world was not going to make a silly, time-wasting detour just to placate irrational animosities.

There was less than four hours to coordinate the first-ever direct flight from Saudi Arabia to Israel, and the team used nearly all of that time to jump through the necessary hoops to make the short flight happen. But while the logistics were complicated, the request was simple: the president of the United States wanted to fly directly from one ally in the region to another. The foreign policy think tanks would have presented every reason why it had never been done before, but not a single good reason why it couldn't be done now.

By contrast, no-nonsense thinking drove the entire Middle East policy team in the Trump administration. Perhaps the most important influence was Jared Kushner, a person unique for his combination of access, trust, and breadth of portfolio. He too led a vigorous push for the unambiguous elevation of the U.S.-Israel relationship. With his team, he served as a force multiplier for the White House's agenda. Jason Greenblatt was the president's special representative for international negotiations until November 2019, when Avi Berkowitz filled that position, playing a critical role in the Peace to Prosperity Vision and the Abraham Accords. Mike Pompeo, the secretary of state beginning in April 2018, was another key player, as were Robert O'Brien, the national security advisor, and Vice President Mike Pence. Steven Mnuchin, the treasury secretary, became one of the greatest champions of the U.S.-Israel relationship and an enormous asset in the establishment and implementation of the Abraham Accords. During the first two years of the Trump administration, Nikki Haley promoted America First policies as ambassador to the United Nations, and she let the world know that the United States would not stand for the bullying heaped on our ally Israel. I got the opportunity to work closely with Ambassador Haley's team, which was led by Jon Lerner, and I learned a lot from him.

It is reasonable to say that any one of the president's senior appointees would have been the strongest advocate for the U.S.-Israel relationship in any past administration. Strong proponents of the relationship were found not only in the State and Defense departments and the intelligence agencies, but also in the Treasury, Energy, Homeland Security, Commerce, and Transportation departments. Beyond the president's appointed personnel, their teams also took the relationship seriously.

There were about fifteen people working for the principals of the Middle East peace team. I cannot imagine another scenario that would have brought together this unique and interesting group of individuals. Every one of the principals that I worked for and every member of the staff that I worked with were among the most talented people I've met, whether in government or the private sector. Of course they had egos and personality quirks, as we all do, but every one of them labored tirelessly to improve America's standing in the world and advance the national interest. The pressure on everyone was immense at pretty much all times, but there was comradery, trust, and complete dedication to changing the dynamics of the Middle East. As a result, nothing of consequence ever leaked—an astonishing feat that perhaps merits a Guinness World Record. Normally the federal government leaks like a sieve, and the Trump administration was particularly prone to internal sabotage from career bureaucrats and, alas, political appointees as well.

I sat in on over two hundred meetings with some combination of the principals in the Middle East peace team. The clear messaging, the goal-oriented conversations, and even body language gave everyone the feeling that transformational opportunities were just around the corner. I also sat in on hundreds of meetings with career diplomats. Virtually every one was more professionally run, but the discussions were stilted, the body language formal, and the impression conveyed was that progress remained elusive.

One of the most refreshing aspects of working in the Trump administration was that the infrastructure of the U.S. government treated us like summer interns. The message was rarely subtle: You're here today, gone tomorrow, so we'll try to minimize the damage you can do. Ambassador Friedman took this not as an obstacle, but rather as a spur to make the most of every day.

Being a political appointee rather than a career diplomat, Friedman had a certain advantage. Tom Cotton spoke to me about the differences between politically appointed ambassadors and career diplomats when I first met him in 2014, while he was in the House of Representatives. He mentioned that on his visits to Asia, the South Koreans always complained that they did not receive political ambassadors as often as the Japanese. Cotton told me that other nations appreciate the professionalism of career diplomats, but when something really needs to get done, you want someone who can go immediately to the secretary of state or even the president. A person who has been personally appointed by the president usually has a far greater ability to go straight to the top.

This principle was illustrated by three ambassadors: David Friedman, from the United States to Israel; Ron Dermer, from Israel to the United States; and Yousef Al Otaiba, from the United Arab Emirates to the United States. They were not regarded as highly trained in international diplomacy, but I would argue that these men will be remembered as three of the most influential ambassadors in history. They are bright, funny, kind, and prophetic. But their greatest asset as diplomats was unfettered access to the ultimate decision maker in their own country. Each gained absolute trust from the top: Friedman with President

Trump, Dermer with Prime Minister Benjamin Netanyahu, and Al Otaiba with Sheikh Mohammed bin Zayed. They were able to have forthright conversations that had immediate value and exponential future value.

5

PEACE OR PROCESS?

From the 1990s until 2017, "the Middle East peace process" defined policy in the region. The operative word was not "peace" but rather "process," the interminable activity that keeps career bureaucrats feeling safe and warm. The "peace process" began with the Oslo Accords signed by the government of Israel and the leadership of the Palestine Liberation Organization in 1993 and 1995. The PLO agreed to recognize the State of Israel formally, while Israel agreed to allow the Palestinians to have limited self-governance in Gaza and the West Bank. The Oslo Accords were regarded as a step toward a formal peace treaty, but the process that followed from it has not brought peace any closer. Instead, the Palestinians have become entrenched in unrealistic positions, while Israelis face more danger.

The Oslo Accords gave rise to a massive cottage industry of "peace processors," including career bureaucrats, members of NGOs, think tankers, academics, and others whose livelihoods revolve around promoting peaceful coexistence in the Middle East. I will assume that all of these people are well intentioned, yet for all the millions of hours and billions of dollars spent on the "peace process," the goal of actual peace became more elusive. Most of the professional processors concluded that the fault lay not with themselves or their process, but with Israeli leadership (i.e., Benjamin Netanyahu and Likud), U.S. foreign policy (i.e., the Iraq war), and meddling regional actors (i.e., Qatar and the UAE). The absence of discernible success from all the time and resources poured into program after program, year after year, did not stop the leaders of peace organizations and think tanks from scoffing at Trump's peace team. Their dismissiveness revealed a lack of self-awareness concerning the failure of their own efforts.

In nearly every meeting I had with them for the first eighteen months of my tenure, the peace processors tried to get me to persuade Ambassador Friedman and Jared Kushner that the next soccer game between Israelis and Arabs would herald peace, that just one more Fulbright Scholarship would provide leadership for real negotiations, etc., etc. I am still moved by the hopefulness of the processors, but I often shared a story that acknowledges their sincerity while illustrating its limitations.

A father and son were walking along the beach when they came upon thousands of starfish washed up on the shore, doomed to dry up and die. The father began picking up a starfish every few steps and tossing it back into the sea. After some time, the son looked up at his father with downcast eyes and said, "Dad, see how many starfish there are, and how fast the sun is going down. You won't be able to make a difference." The father bent down, picked up another starfish, threw it back into the sea, and then replied, "I made a difference for that one."

Each starfish saved is a saved starfish, as the father pointed out. Likewise, each Middle East program that can foster goodwill is a worthy endeavor (though I don't think they should all necessarily be funded by the American taxpayers). But unless you can significantly change the dynamics of the system, you will still have an unsolved problem at the end of the day.

The processors themselves do not seem to have confidence that their approach is really changing the dynamics. I spoke with well over a hundred different peace-processor organizations, and nearly every conversation had a similar ending. I asked them to describe the project of which they were proudest. They would do so with great eloquence and enthusiasm. I congratulated them on their efforts and passion, then asked if they could introduce me to ten up-and-coming leaders they had been cultivating. The reply would typically be: "Let me check to see if they'd be willing to meet with you," or, "I'm not sure they are ready for this next step yet, but as soon as they are, I'll call you." I still have not received a single phone call about the next generation of leaders. I have not received a call from any alumnus of the many peace process groups that the U.S. government has funded to the tune of hundreds of millions of dollars, saying, "Hey, Aryeh! Let's sit down and come up with a broad-based solution for all people in the region." The obvious conclusion is that no new generation of leaders is being cultivated. And that is because every one of our programs has been grounded in unrealistic goals.

Up to now, the focus of our Middle East policy has been on a process that wasn't getting anywhere, in the name of goals that are not realistic. There will never be a two-state solution based upon the Green Line—the 1949 armistice line between Israel and Jordan, or the pre-1967 border—with minimal, mutually agreed land swaps. Objective observers know it, yet the "process" supposedly leading there has continued for decades. This is a foreign policy steeped in naïveté. Billions of dollars and millions of people-hours have been wasted on unachievable goals.

The Trump peace team started with some elementary principles. First, do no harm, *primum non nocere*, the bedrock principle of the Hippocratic Oath. Second, if the current model isn't working, stop using it and come up with a model that has a better chance of success. Third, if you're going to work hard toward a goal, it should be both possible to achieve and worth the effort.

6

LEVELING UP

Before I first arrived at the U.S. Embassy in Tel Aviv, I had
fantastic visions of helicopters and motorcades, secret meetings, and high-level international intrigue. Then reality set in.
First, there was the jet lag. My family were all disoriented by the
transatlantic move. What's more, the rhythm of the embassy
wasn't calibrated for a senior advisor to the ambassador. I found
that Ambassador Friedman was off to an excellent start, however. He had already succeeded in winning over large parts of
the embassy staff. It was clear that he had attained the full faith
and confidence of President Trump and the rest of the White
House. He had also developed a good rapport with Prime Minister Netanyahu and his team.

As for myself, I figured I could at least be charming and
personable, so I decided to go around to the myriad embassy
branches and introduce myself as a conduit to the front office
(the ambassador and his senior team). I was ceaselessly impressed
by the sense of duty I saw among the Americans who staff our
embassies around the world. They hail from all fifty states and all
U.S. territories as well. They come from different backgrounds and
cultures, and they have traveled to many countries to represent

our nation. I am certain that many of my embassy colleagues in Israel were politically and ideologically on the opposite side from myself, but I respect them for having committed a substantial portion of their lives to the career of foreign service, and I admire their families for their sacrifice.

I shook hands in every branch of the embassy, received briefings, and tried to listen more than talk. But as an entrepreneur in spirit and a deal junky by career, I couldn't help myself when I met with the Commercial Service team. The job of the people who work there is to win business opportunities for American firms abroad. The Commercial Service was then located a bit more than half a mile south of the main embassy campus, on the boardwalk that lines Tel Aviv's beautiful beach. My introductory meeting with staff in the seaside conference room began like all the others, with polite small talk. "So, where are you from?" they asked. "Who are you here with?" "What tour of duty is this for you?" I'll be the first to admit that working on the beach in Tel Aviv is not the biggest hardship tour in the world.

After the pleasantries had concluded, I learned that there weren't many American companies playing competitively in the field in Israel. Once I decided that I had learned enough, I asked what major deals had been done in Israel over the previous five years, what U.S. companies bid on them, and whether they had won. I also asked for the same data for Chinese companies. I then said something to this effect: "While we're not fortune tellers, many countries of course plan their large infrastructure projects years in advance. What are the deals that will be out there in the four years that Ambassador Friedman will be chief of mission? And which U.S. companies should be bidding on them?" I thought those were innocuous questions and expected the answers to come in handy before long. The Commercial Service people said they didn't have the information handy, but promised to do the research and get back to me ASAP.

It took maybe twenty minutes to walk back up the boardwalk to the main embassy campus. It couldn't have been less than 100 degrees outside, and I was going to need a shower before I interacted with anyone else. Glancing at my watch, I remembered that I needed to be on a secure conference call very soon, so I picked up the pace and then sprinted up the stairs, sweating even more. As I turned the corner to enter my office, I heard an unmistakable voice call out "Aryeh!" It was the deputy chief of mission (DCM). I pivoted on my heels and walked into her office instead.

"Hi! What's going on?" I asked.

I was invited to sit down on one of the uncomfortable blue couches in the office. I had déjà vu, recalling a time in middle school when I was called into the principal's office and didn't know what I had done wrong. But I knew that I was about to receive a lecture.

It started with a question: "Do you know what your title at the embassy is?"

That sounds simple enough, but in my case it was complicated. Ambassador Friedman had wanted me to be his chief of staff, but the State Department was not excited about that, because a chief of staff is ostensibly in charge of staff. The State Department was much more comfortable with the title "Senior Advisor." An advisor is a person who offers advice to someone willing or interested to hear it. My full title was "Senior Advisor to the Ambassador," which limited my advice-giving range to my boss. That might seem trivial, but in the realm of government, and especially diplomacy, words matter a lot, including the words in titles. As a senior advisor, I was most certainly not in charge of anything, and I didn't really have an official connection to anyone other than the person to whom I was assigned to give advice.

Sensing where the DCM was going with her question, I stepped out in front of the issue and said that I was "Senior Advisor to the Ambassador to Israel, David Friedman."

The DCM sarcastically congratulated me for knowing my title, and then asked, "Why in the world did you think you could ask the Commercial Service team to prepare a report for you?" It was not my role to be assigning work to other people in the embassy, she informed me. "Your job is to meet people, learn about what they do, and be prepared to answer questions that the ambassador may have for you. But it is explicitly not within your purview to assign anyone any task unless the ambassador or I directly request you to make the ask on our behalf."

At that moment I wondered why I had moved my family across the ocean just to serve as something slightly less practical than a fax machine.

I stewed about the conversation much more than I should have for the next three hours or so. I couldn't wait to address the issue with Friedman, who is first and foremost a friend and a mentor. He often allowed me to ride home with him at the end of the day, and on this particular day he must have seen the smoke coming out of my ears as I began venting my annoyance. He imparted some wisdom before I really had a chance to shove my foot into my mouth.

"Everything that happens, happens for a reason," he counseled. "We are here at a unique time in history, and we can accomplish more for the U.S.-Israel relationship than you can even imagine. We just cannot make any mistakes." He continued, "Aryeh, you are correct to want the information you asked for, but every time you open your mouth, people in the embassy and in the government of Israel don't think it's Aryeh Lightstone speaking. They think it's the ambassador of the United States speaking through his senior advisor. Keep that in mind, because it is relevant to every conversation you have. And while you might not think people care much about who you are or what you do, people are out to make sure we don't succeed. Even worse, they're out to make sure that we fail, and fail spectacularly."

I took several deep breaths. I had been humbled. This was a lesson I was to learn over and over: I could have things my way and possibly hurt the mission, or I could swallow my pride and work on making sure the mission remained the priority. As a serial entrepreneur who did not have a long history of taking direction, I was going to find this a challenge. Fortunately, Friedman kept me informed of his goals and how they were to be achieved, and if you believe in a goal, you will make sacrifices to achieve it. As one of my Emirati friends put it, "When you are in a war, you can sleep in a trench."

My outreach to the Commercial Service did return some value a few weeks later. Steven Mnuchin, the secretary of the treasury, came to Israel on October 26 for his first of many visits. Many embassies around the world consider themselves lucky to receive one cabinet visit over a four-year period. The U.S. Embassy in Israel averaged one cabinet-level visit every six weeks for the duration of the Trump administration. Such visits are highly scripted and well orchestrated. This was especially true in the case of Secretary Mnuchin, who is quite detail-oriented. He or his senior staff signed off on every meeting in the schedule.

During the preparation for this visit, I was able to level up in the embassy. I knew some of Mnuchin's staff, and they kept me in the loop on the planning. Several members of the embassy team came to see me as a useful go-between to enhance communication and maximize the benefits of the trip. While my part in the planning helped me gain esteem in the eyes of some of my new colleagues, it did not get me into any of the big meetings.

When senior people in government travel, they bring along their teams. The embassy plans the entire trip, with guidance from Washington. Traditionally, when cabinet secretaries go to meet with their counterpart in another country, they bring their chief of staff and two or three assistant secretaries, and then the ambassador will join the meeting on behalf of the embassy. Some visitors from Washington, cabinet level and above, will meet with officials of the country and not even include the ambassador in the meetings. Friedman didn't know every U.S. cabinet member, but he made it very clear that he was in charge of the U.S.-Israel relationship on behalf of the president, and therefore no visitors from Washington to Israel would meet with Israeli government officials if he was not present.

The fighting that occurs in the background to get into the meetings when senior government officials visit is a sight to behold. A lady named Edna in the Israeli Prime Minister's Office decides who gets into what meeting and where everyone will sit. While I personally believe it apocryphal, many people told me that she has overruled prime ministers and visiting foreign ministers. "Don't mess with Edna," I heard. I am grateful that Edna and I got off on the right foot during Mnuchin's first visit. I did not make the manifest for the meeting in the prime minister's fabled conference room, but I did merit a ride in the motorcade to the Prime Minister's Office and a hangout with other senior staff in the vestibule.

After a while, to my surprise, I was summoned into the conference room. I was told that the meeting had been going well when Secretary Mnuchin asked Prime Minister Netanyahu about how U.S. companies were doing in winning tenders in Israel, and if they were not, why not, and about how Chinese companies were doing, especially with the Haifa port tender prominently featured in the news. Ambassador Friedman replied, "Lightstone has this information." This helped to give me a specific project to focus on that could provide added value for Friedman.

Like most opportunities, this one was a double-edged sword. By being called into the meeting for information that was needed, I was further elevated, I believed, in the eyes of my colleagues and friends, and most importantly the ambassador. I also became, de facto, the American voice for the success of American companies in Israel. It was a role I would relish, but also a daunting one. At the conclusion of the meeting, Mnuchin told Friedman how great it was that his "political guy" (meaning me) was going to bring immediate value to President Trump's priority of countering Chinese influence while helping American companies prosper internationally. I was overwhelmed, to say the least.

That experience during Mnuchin's visit was my first major professional highlight. It gave me credibility with our embassy team, the Prime Minister's Office, and the Treasury Department. It was also during this visit that I became part of a team with Edna and Orit, the person in charge of foreign visits from North America at the Prime Minister's Office. One might have thought it was Netanyahu's chief of staff, his foreign policy advisor, his head of national security, or his military secretary that I needed to win over, but it was really Edna and Orit. The two of them decided the most important aspects of high-level visits from the United States—the landing of private planes, the security package that VIPs received, the hotels that dignitaries stayed in, the food they were served, the meetings they had, and who else got into the meetings.

The three of us planned and executed over fifty high-level delegation visits. We coordinated to wrestle with our respective bureaucracies, and hand in hand we made sure that visits ran so smoothly that leadership had the time, space, and energy to elevate the U.S.-Israel relationship to heights not previously imagined. We laughed together. We yelled at each other. Nearly every visit was followed by a wheels-up party in which the first several minutes were spent in apologies for things said in the heat of the moment.

7

ABSOLUTELY STARVING

In my third week at the embassy, I was becoming exhausted by midafternoon because I had been working both U.S. and Israeli hours dealing with some issues in Washington regarding State Department reports. I found it challenging to contend with the bureaucracy in D.C. and the complex politics of the Middle East, but I also felt some guilt over what my wife went through every morning to get our four children to school with all their homework, school supplies, and lunches. While I rode with the ambassador and his security detail to Tel Aviv from Herzliya, the location of our temporary home, Estee braved the traffic to drive the children to four different schools in Raanana, where we would be moving in October. I don't think the ambassador needed the security detail as much as Estee needed a support team to cajole my crying kids to go to schools where they didn't yet really know anyone in their second week and didn't know the language or culture particularly well.

On Tuesday afternoon that week I was in a skiff (a room without any electronics) talking with Elizabeth Richard, the U.S. ambassador to Lebanon. We were discussing the Lebanese-Israeli maritime border dispute as well as the ongoing political crisis in Lebanon and Hezbollah's growing missile arsenal. It was a very serious conversation, and I was listening intently to everything our heroic ambassador in Beirut was saying. That may not have been Ambassador Richard's impression, as I was yawning every thirty seconds or so. My mind was alert, but my body was failing to look awake. Then the senior marine at the embassy, affectionately called Gunny, entered the skiff and interrupted our secure video call. That was an astonishing action, jolting me out of my nodding state. I asked Gunny what was going on, and he told me that my daughter's school had called the embassy's emergency number and said she was being starved, though he was dubious. Gunny said that the marine who took the call couldn't really understand what the lady from the school was saying, but he thought I should phone over there immediately because she sounded distressed.

I ran out to find my cell phone and saw ten missed calls from my daughter Shayna's school. This was strange, because the school was only to call me in an emergency. I called back and spoke to the secretary, introducing myself as Shayna's father and asking if everything was okay. The secretary responded in a very loud voice, "Shayna is absolutely starving!" Then, after a dramatic pause, "She forgot her lunch." I realized that I had been holding my breath only when I finally exhaled in relief and burst into laughter. I had just run out of a secure call with our ambassador in Beirut, who was facing great challenges there day in and day out. because my daughter's school's secretary called the embassy emergency number to say in broken English that Shayna Lightstone was starving because she hadn't brought her lunch.

In the postmortem, I reminded Shayna's school never to call the embassy emergency number unless it was a real emergency. My children learned pretty quickly that I didn't have just a regular job and they couldn't call me at work and claim an emergency when they didn't pack their lunch to school. And from that moment on, whenever I saw Gunny he winked and asked, "How is peanut butter doing today?" Peanut butter became Shayna's code name among the embassy marines.

8

NGO ECHO CHAMBER

My role of senior advisor to the ambassador was unprecedented at the embassy when I joined the team, and some people in leadership wanted to define it as narrowly as they could. Going along with the institutional leadership would have been easier for Ambassador Friedman, but he knew that he wanted me to be a force multiplier for him if he was going to accomplish his objectives. He is supremely effective when he focuses on one particular initiative, but he would be the first person to tell you he is a poor multitasker. My most important function was to take as much day-to-day work as possible off his plate so he could concentrate on his history-making primary goals. Friedman and I set about to fill my days with productive work until we carved out the proper niche for my skills.

As the resident rabbi at the embassy, one thing I was well qualified to do was explain all things Orthodox Jewish to anyone who was interested. Beyond that, I expected that one of my responsibilities would be penning some white papers and writing key speeches for the ambassador on issues we both cared deeply about—Jerusalem, the Golan Heights, Jewish unity, and supporting Israel as an American value, among others. I remember my first attempt to put words to paper on Friedman's behalf. I have never been an excellent writer, but I was proud of the product that I put in front of him. I had worked hard on it and believed it made his points in a manner and style that he would use. After just a few minutes, he let me know that he would pencil in some comments. I was pleased, expecting him to do some light editing. I figured that I had found a path forward for myself and that I would soon be providing real value to the mission.

Fifteen minutes later, David politely called me back to his office to read his comments. They weren't comments, though. He had completely rewritten the speech, and it was light years better than anything I could ever have written. I had known that he was a persuasive litigator and able with a pen. At that moment I also knew that I would not be writing any more speeches for him. He was just too good for me to add significant value, so our roles reversed. He would draft speeches as well as articles, and then send them to me for comments and suggestions.

That wasn't going to fill my days, however, so it was back to the drawing board to figure out what else I should do. An enormous amount of embassy workflow is dictated by presidential priorities and timing. Big visits by officials require a lot of preparation and follow-up. Every U.S. Embassy is required to draft reports on host countries in certain subjects of concern, which the State Department then uses to compile the annual country reports mandated by Congress. The embassy reports incorporate information provided by government officials, religious groups, nongovernmental organizations, human rights monitors, journalists, and academics. Before Ambassador Friedman's arrival, certain reports on Israel, particularly the Human Rights Report and the International Religious Freedom Report, had served to perpetuate a cycle of failure in the Middle East. Friedman wanted to change that.

On the surface, at least, it seems sensible for the U.S. gov-ernment to have some idea of how other countries, both allies and adversaries, are performing with respect to such important concerns as human rights and religious freedom. I'm sure that Congress didn't intend that these mandatory reports would end up manufacturing a self-congratulatory industry of NGOs and donors whose work reinforces prejudice against Israel and the Jewish people, but that's what transpired. As a result, the embassy in Israel has an officer dedicated exclusively to these reports. Throughout the year, that person meets with the groups that conduct the research that goes into the lengthy reports on human rights and religious freedom.

The reporting by NGOs goes into the embassy's official report on Israel, and then into the State Department's annual country reports, which policymakers in Congress, the State Department, and the White House use to make real-world decisions. NGO reports are also echoed by left-leaning news outlets. The NGOs quoted in the State Department reports then go back to their donors—whether foundations, private individuals, or national governments—and say, "Look! The U.S. has included us in their official policy papers. Our work is essential to shaping policy." So they receive more funding, publish more reports, and get included in further embassy reports. This cycle yields unintended consequences for our national interest, but consequences very much intended by the NGOs.

I do not have any experience with these reports aside from the ones generated by the U.S. Embassy in Israel and the for-mer U.S. Consulate in Jerusalem. It is possible that the issues I'm describing are not unique to Israel. But I can say that in the case of Israel these embassy reports have created an echo chamber of bad ideas, leading to bad policy, which reinforces the bad ideas, and so on. When Israel was unable to meet the demands made by policymakers in D.C., the next round of NGO reports would show Israel to be falling short, and the vicious cycle would continue. This has led to a focus on issues that are deemed urgent by outside organizations at the expense of issues that are actually important to reducing conflict. The fact is that Israeli violence against Israeli Arabs and Palestinians is constantly condemned by every stream and strain of Israeli leadership, while the Palestinian practice of pay-for-slay gets little notice, even though it shows terrorism to be a feature and not a bug in the Palestinian system.

One way that these official reports are harmful to America's allies, including Israel, is by turning those counties' openness against them, in an ironic twist. The more freedom a country offers, the easier it is for NGOs to report on it. Israel's extensive freedoms and robust rule of law permit NGOs to operate freely and report without fear, so the State Department reports include voluminous complaints about Israel. By contrast, practically no research is conducted in Gaza, which is run by Hamas. If NGOs did operate in Gaza, they might have to report that they themselves had become victims of imprisonment or worse. So there is damnation by volume against Israel, but near silence on abuses in Gaza.

The State Department claims that the West Bank, which is controlled by the supposedly moderate Palestinian Authority, allows NGOs to work and report freely. That is true to an extent, but State performs inelegant loops and dives in making its case. If an NGO reports exclusively through the lens of Israeli "apartheid" and "occupation," it will be respected and welcomed back into the Palestinian-controlled territories. But if an NGO speaks about the innumerable human rights abuses and the lack of religious freedom in those territories, its welcome will be extremely short-lived.

The Palestinian-controlled territories command but a few pages in the reports, covering only a handful of cases. At the same time, there are dozens upon dozens of pages condemning and denouncing Israel in excruciating detail. Israel is not given an opportunity to respond to the allegations before the embassy reports go out. Moreover, the reporting lacks a modicum of context and sources are not independently verified. Yet the United States government relies upon these reports in forging policy. The reports that come out of the State Department are read by thousands of people in government, academia, think tanks, and media. Their content is amplified in analysis and commentary, influencing how the public thinks about the region.

Ambassador Friedman was determined to confront the nefarious moral relativism that had been baked into those embassy reports. As the chief of mission, he needed to sign off on the reports personally before they left the embassy, and he tasked me with overhauling them first. He knew it wasn't going to be thrilling or glamorous work. Crafting reports doesn't involve helicopter rides or motorcades. But it was important work, as it would play a role in shaping perceptions and policy.

For the better part of forty-five days, I pored over every report that had left the embassy over the prior decade, as well as those that had been drafted for the upcoming year. I noticed that nearly every one of those reports was some form of boilerplate from the year before. Names and numbers had changed, but the tone and narration had not. And as they say, if you do what you've always done, you'll get what you've always gotten.

I knew that my colleagues were bright, eager, and not at all enthused about simply inserting data from NGO websites into official U.S. government reports. Over the course of a month, we sat down together and rewrote the reports as best as possible. We began with a frank disclaimer that basically said: While

Congress mandates that we include publicly available reporting, it is clear that there is bias in reporting that involves Israel and the Palestinian-controlled territories, and we at the embassy cannot independently verify any of the specifics.

Then we made changes in terminology. Past reports would refer generally to "NGOs" and use wiggle phrases like "NGOs state that...." We began the practice of naming specific NGOs, and changing words that connote certainty, like "state," to "claim" or "allege," which appropriately indicate the subjectivity of the content. These changes enabled readers to look up the NGOs and learn about their funders, and also conveyed the point that NGOs don't speak on behalf of anyone but themselves. Among other changes in language, we eliminated the term "illegally occupied Palestinian territory." We changed "the West Bank" to "the disputed territories." Besides changing the whole tenor of the reports, we also recategorized the reports to include Jerusalem as part of Israel.

This obscure endeavor may seem way down in the weeds, but Ambassador Friedman was not going to leave any part of U.S.-Israel policy to chance. If a report was going to leave the embassy while he was chief of mission, it would reflect the Trump administration's policies. These reports sent a warning shot to the NGOs and their funders: They could not expect their bias to be simply regurgitated for official U.S. consumption, and they would no longer be setting policy on their own agenda.

This new approach to the reports also enfranchised our team at the embassy. They fought over every paragraph in every report, zealous to produce better reports. They enjoyed the process of looking at the material handed to them with fresh eyes and through a new lens. As for myself, I still didn't feel that I was reaching my potential at the embassy, but I did feel that I was beginning to serve as an effective bridge between the ambassador, the embassy reporting staff, and the State Department.

9

DON'T YIELD AN INCH

A mbassador Friedman's top agenda item was to bring closure to the Jerusalem Embassy Act, but meanwhile another issue came up that also involved an existing U.S. law, and the principle of not yielding an inch to adversaries. Under the Anti-Terrorism Act of 1987, passed by a wide bipartisan margin, the Palestinian Liberation Organization could not maintain its diplomatic mission in Washington, D.C., if the Palestinians pursued action against the State of Israel in the International Criminal Court. The ICC believes it has authority even over countries that have not signed an agreement allowing it to have jurisdiction over them. The United States, Israel, and many of our allies have robust judicial systems, and there is no reason to allow our government or citizens to be subject to a court system that we have no control over and is not answerable to any of us.

One morning in November 2017, a senior officer at the embassy in Tel Aviv came running into my office at about 8:15 with his hair still damp from the shower he took after riding his bicycle to work. Mark and I enjoyed each other's company, but probably did not agree on a single policy issue. He held a memo that was going out of the embassy to the State Department recommending that the secretary of state certify to Congress that the Palestinian Authority was in compliance with the legal requirements to maintain a mission in Washington. Dozens of people are involved in researching, writing, and editing such memos, which must then be cleared by embassy officials before arriving on the secretary of state's desk. This particular memo already had sixteen signatures on it.

Mark asked if I had heard the speech by Mahmoud Abbas, president of the Palestinian Authority, to the United Nations General Assembly in September. I replied that I had read some notes on it but had not actually heard the speech. "Let's watch it," he said, pulling it up on my computer. We listened from start to finish. "So?" he asked, allowing me to reach my own conclusion.

It was very clear from the speech that the PA was or would be actively using the International Criminal Court to pursue Israel in every way it could. This wasn't supposition. It was the president of the Palestinian Authority speaking plain as day on the world's largest stage. Yet sixteen people had signed a memo recommending that the secretary of state certify the exact opposite to Congress. I thanked Mark, and he said, "I'm just doing my job." (Indeed, like countless other career foreign service officers, he carried out his job with professionalism and excellence.) I knew that we needed to change the memo, so Mark and I brought it to the ambassador's office.

Walking into his executive suite on that day, I knew he would be thrilled that his team had uncovered this policy flaw in time for it to be corrected, but also annoyed because dealing with this issue would be a distraction from his primary focus, which was to begin the application of the Jerusalem Embassy Act. Every issue pertaining to Israel, the Palestinians, and the broader region went to the Oval Office, and nearly every decision involved the president, while the few that did not certainly involved Kushner,

Pompeo, Friedman, Berkowitz, and others. The leadership from Friedman all the way to D.C. made big, bold decisions, but tried not to overwhelm the system with too many issues. That is why the people tasked with the Middle East file didn't want to use up time and bandwidth on the Palestinian mission. Its presence was not a driving factor in anyone's decision-making calculus. Friedman and Kushner didn't think that closing it would necessarily be beneficial. In fact, there was a belief that the mission could be helpful as the president pursued what he called the Deal of the Century.

But when I showed the memo to Friedman, within thirty seconds he said that he must speak immediately with Rex Tillerson, the secretary of state. Normally when an ambassador wants to discuss a memo with a secretary of state, there would be a memo about why the ambassador would want to speak to the secretary, and that memo itself would need to work its way to the top of the State Department before the phone call could be arranged. But David Friedman was no traditional ambassador, and when he said he wanted to speak to Secretary Tillerson, I literally ran to the front-office team and got the machinery moving. The phone call happened that same day, vastly quicker than any other memo-focused call between an ambassador and a secretary of state would come about, if not as fast as Friedman wanted. He told Tillerson that while he should do as he saw fit, the facts on the issue were clear-cut. "If I were your lawyer," he said, "I would not recommend certifying something to Congress that is clearly and demonstrably false."

Meanwhile I was trying to get Jason Greenblatt on the other line so the White House would know about the Friedman-Tillerson phone call. Friedman was already game-planning how the issue would affect his strategy for the Jerusalem recognition, for which he would be flying to Washington in a matter of days.

There is a frenetic energy in the air while decisions of this magnitude are being made, and then an eerie silence afterward. I sat with David in his office overlooking the Mediterranean Sea, waiting for the repercussions. As he replayed the conversation and his decision-making process, he was back in legal mode, and to me there was nothing more educational. His powers of reason and persuasion are second to none, and his unique ability to plan for every contingency is awe-inspiring. Friedman went through a list of people one by one: When will they find out? What will they say? Whom will they say it to? What can go wrong? For a riveting ninety minutes I listened, took notes, and played devil's advocate.

It would have been easier to indulge the Palestinian Authority and allow the mission to remain open. But a law is a law, and this administration was determined to set rules and ramifications, and to follow through. Classic D.C. thinking since the Oslo Accords has been that the Palestinian Authority are the moderates, the peacemakers, and the vehicle for good in the region. I don't believe it was ever true, and it was most certainly not accurate when Friedman and I were in our embassy offices. It is possible, or even likely, that they are better than any of the other immediate alternatives in the region, but that certainly doesn't make them good. For too long they were coddled to the point that they didn't believe that rules and norms would ever apply to them, and indeed until the Trump administration came around, they did not.

The Israeli ambassador to the United States, Ron Dermer, was fond of pointing out that the Palestinians have never won a war but never lost a negotiation. The PA strategy was to negotiate for maximum concessions from Israel and extract those concessions in exchange for promises to be fulfilled later by the PA. The Palestinians would then walk away from the table, returning months or years later and starting from the last Israeli concessions, but also from the original beginning point for PA concessions. Even though the concessions were rarely codified as a formal agreement, it was taken for granted at each subsequent negotiation that Israel's new opening bid would be their final bid from the previous negotiation. The PA position got stronger while Israel's grew weaker, and these positions gradually became internationally accepted. The Palestinians didn't live up to their agreements or even pretend to, but if the Israelis couldn't or wouldn't live up to their end, the entire peace-process enterprise kicked into high gear to condemn Israel, and those condemnations would make their way into U.S. Embassy reports. This became a conflict waged in the halls of international bodies and on the editorial pages of key newspapers in capitals across the world. The time and attention focused on this particular conflict grew out of proportion to every other conflict in the world. Facts on the ground came to matter far less than the court of public opinion, and in that court, Israel was losing badly.

For progress to happen in the Middle East, rules and norms must apply to all players in the region. If the Palestinians were pursuing actions against Israel in the International Criminal Court, we could not look the other way or disregard U.S. law. When the mission was closed on September 13, 2018, the message communicated to Ramallah (the seat of the PA government) was that we would no longer wink at Palestinian violations just because they are perceived as the underdog. We would hold them to a higher standard. Taking this stance was necessary to regain the self-respect and deterrence capacity that had been frittered away in the previous eight years of apologies and capitulation. Following through on one specific law gave a clear guideline to the Palestinians, and to many others in the region as well.

In response, the head of the Palestinian mission in D.C., Husam Zomlot, told the AFP, "It was unsurprising to us the Trump administration gave us only two choices: either we lose our relationship with the administration or we lose our rights as a nation." He continued, "Our president, leadership and the people of Palestine opted for our rights."* This might sound like a wonderful declaration from a freedom fighter, but it is completely detached from reality. The U.S. Congress passed a law imposing conditions for keeping a Palestinian mission open in Washington, and the Trump administration enforced that law. The Palestinians failed to acknowledge that the United States has a right to legislate requirements they must meet in order to operate in the nation's capital. They were offended by that law and believed that their feelings should hold sway in the American court of public opinion, which was preposterous.

---

* AFP, "Palestinian mission shuttered in Washington," *Yahoo! News*, September 13, 2018.

IO

RECOGNIZING JERUSALEM

President Trump made a campaign promise to move our embassy to Jerusalem. Like his predecessors, he signed the waiver of the Jerusalem Embassy Act on June 1, and a few days later the U.S. Senate passed a resolution 90-0 reaffirming the law. Politicians make many promises while running for office, and then once they arrive in office they find it difficult or inconvenient to follow through. One of the most persuasive arguments that David Friedman made to the president about recognizing Jerusalem and moving the embassy was that if he didn't keep the promise he made on the campaign trail he would be "just another politician." This was anathema to the president, and while he would not make the decision on that basis alone, he certainly did not take kindly to being told he would be considered just another politician.

Ambassador Friedman kept U.S. hours for the entire months of October, November, and December in 2017, and did likewise off and on during his term as ambassador. He let people in Washington know that there was never a moment that they couldn't reach him if they were having a conversation relevant to Israel. This was to ensure that distance did not create daylight. I worked at the embassy during normal daytime hours, between 7:30 a.m. and 4:00 p.m., and then went to the ambassador's residence with all items that he needed to be briefed on.

Friedman knew that the key decisions about implementing the Jerusalem Embassy Act were going to be made in Washington. Most ambassadors are allowed to be away from the country to which they are assigned for a limited amount of time, but Friedman took most rules as little more than suggestions. In early November, he basically told me to keep an eye on the embassy and make sure that nothing went wrong while he was away. He planned a one-week stay in Washington, but it stretched into four weeks. During that time, he repositioned me from being the person editing State Department reports, to being the primary point of contact between himself and the embassy. In the world of diplomacy, current information is the coin of the realm, so I now entered a position of greater responsibility. I worked Israeli hours and was also on call for the ambassador during all U.S. work hours. It was an exhausting and exhilarating time.

When Friedman returned to Israel at the beginning of December, he summoned the deputy chief of mission and me to his home for an emergency briefing and let us know that the president would be recognizing Jerusalem as the capital of Israel on December 6, just a few days away. I didn't know whether to laugh or cry. Joy at the news was washing over me, but so was panic in view of the work that needed to be done very quickly. In truth, there was no time for laughter or tears. The embassy had to change its security posture. Governor Rick Scott of Florida happened to be coming to town shortly, as governors do from time to time, and his visit involved a logistics arrangement of its own, in addition to the slew of issues to be addressed before the big announcement.

It is the job of security professionals to err on the side of caution, and security concerns are closely connected with worries about political reactions in the Middle East. This was a running theme during our time at the embassy. Every move made by President Trump—and enacted by Secretary Pompeo or Ambassador Friedman or Jared Kushner—was met with dire warnings such as, "This will cause havoc and mayhem from Indonesia to Morocco. Death and destruction will abound." This kind of hysteria had deterred previous administrations from making policy decisions that were not morally difficult, but did require courage and perspective. The link between policy and security concerns was made clear during Governor Scott's visit to Israel.

On the evening of December 5, Ambassador Friedman and his wife Tammy hosted a beautiful event for Governor Scott and his wonderful wife and their entire delegation. For major visits like this, the delegations would mingle for about forty-five minutes in the stunning garden of the ambassador's home, overlooking the Mediterranean Sea, while the principals sat in the ambassador's office right off the main entrance, getting acquainted and sharing insights that wouldn't be voiced in a larger group. Gaining access to these private meetings entailed a power struggle, though by this point it was a given that I would be included.

Friedman opened the meeting in his office by thanking Governor Scott for his leadership, then immediately jumped into the president's decision to recognize Jerusalem as the capital and the potential impact it would have on the U.S.-Israel relationship and the region. Governor Scott, an early supporter of Trump and a longtime friend of Israel, was very pleased to hear about the upcoming announcement, and even more pleased to learn that it would happen just two days later, while he was still in Israel.

Then the entire group had dinner in the garden. It was the best type of diplomatic event—a buffet. In the more traditional sit-down dinners you received what I would call a polite portion, which meant you left the table hungry. This was not the case at the informal events that the Friedmans hosted in their garden. The best were old fashioned barbeques, and the next best were the type we enjoyed that evening, with abundant finger food such as spicy salmon rolls and beef spring rolls. The conversation flowed easily, the warm December air was filled with good vibes, and a lot of business was solidified between Israeli and Florida-based companies. Everyone was having a fantastic time.

I was hoping to get some Florida State Trooper coins in exchange for a few of Ambassador Friedman's coins. During my time in the administration, I tried to collect as many challenge coins as possible from visitors to Israel as a reminder of the people I met there. I found swapping coins to be a good icebreaker and a way of offering people a small token of gratitude for their efforts on my behalf. So I sauntered over to the lead of Governor Scott's security detail with some coins to trade. He shook my hand and give me his challenge coin, and then I took the opportunity to explain the significance of the ambassador's coin.

One side of Friedman's challenge coin had the traditional image of U.S. and Israeli flags meeting in the middle. The other side featured the Liberty Bell with the Hebrew words for "Proclaim liberty throughout the land," part of the inscription on the historic bell in Philadelphia. The words come from Leviticus 25:10, and the meaning is self-explanatory. But an added significance emerges if you read the entire verse: "And ye shall hallow the fiftieth year, and proclaim liberty throughout all the land unto all the inhabitants there of." In the biblical cycle of time, the fiftieth year is the Jubilee, when slaves are freed, debts are lifted, and people return to their family's property. Friedman is extremely diligent on the issues dearest to him, and he planned this coin purposefully, with an eye to a fifty-year historical cycle. The idea of the modern State of Israel had its international conception with the Balfour Declaration in 1917. Fifty years later, the Six-Day War occurred, and Israel expanded its borders beyond what had callously been called the "Auschwitz borders," maintained from the founding of Israel in 1948 up until 1967. In that same war, Jerusalem was reunified, with many holy areas including the Western Wall and the Temple Mount coming under Israeli rule for the first time in nearly two thousand years. Friedman designed his challenge coin fifty years later, in 2017, and he had big plans for the year.

By now it was semipublic knowledge that Trump was going to make the announcement recognizing Jerusalem as Israel's capital the next day, and I was thrilled to explain the coin's deeper meaning to someone who knew what was ahead. The governor's security lead was clearly touched by it. He thanked me for our efforts on his team's behalf and wished me well.

"Thank you for coming," I replied. "Thank you for supporting the relationship, and thank you for your service." I then asked, "But are you saying goodbye? I thought you were here at least until December 7."

"We've been told that the threat assessment will be elevated tomorrow," he explained. "We cannot take that type of risk with the governor and First Lady of Florida. We're going to head back tonight." He shook my hand and said "thank you" again.

I was in a bit of a daze. Apparently a lot had gone on while I was playing business matchmaker in the ambassador's garden. Little did any of us know that the embassy security team was having a discussion with the governor's security team as we enjoyed our evening. The governor's delegation was loaded up on the buses and ready to depart when I found Friedman.

"Man, it is disappointing that the governor is leaving early," I said to him. "I'm surprised you didn't convince him otherwise."

He looked at me in shock. "Who is leaving early? No one told me anyone is leaving early."

Without another word, I turned and ran to the security post

at the end of the property and asked the guards to keep the gates shut for a minute. I then ran to the governor's car and asked that he have a word with the ambassador before he left.

"Sure!" he said, not knowing what it was about.

While at least a hundred Floridians were detained in cars and buses, I escorted the governor back into the house.

"Why are you leaving first thing tomorrow morning?" Friedman asked him.

"Your security guys told us it was too dangerous to stay," Scott replied. "I assumed they were delivering a message on your behalf."

The two huddled for about five minutes.

Deliberating on whether to override a security decision would be a common occurrence over the next few years. When you overrule the machinery of government, you assume the responsibility for that decision. When considerations of human life and safety are involved, there is perfectly good reason to be risk-averse.

The ambassador and the governor decided that cutting the visit short would send exactly the wrong message, signaling a lack of resolve. Governor Scott was a big believer in the Jerusalem Embassy Act, in David Friedman, and Donald Trump. Just ninety minutes earlier we had been celebrating the impending announcement of the recognition of Jerusalem as the capital of Israel. But when your security team tells you something, challenging its advice takes backbone.

In this case, however, the security teams were not actually overruled. Instead, Friedman and Scott both called in their teams, and they jointly declared that the governor would complete his scheduled visit in Israel for the sake of good policy. In less than twenty minutes, six of us then rewrote the entire schedule for the Florida delegation to make sure that everyone, including the security teams, was comfortable with the next steps. The security teams didn't exactly high-five us on the way out of the room, but they understood chain of command. They also grasped the policy imperative. So they went to work on making this the safest visit possible.

The next day, December 6, President Trump announced that the United States recognized Jerusalem as the capital of Israel and that he would ask the State Department to begin preparations to move the U.S. Embassy there from Tel Aviv. Those who asked what the United States would get in return missed some important truths. One is that the action simply fulfilled a U.S. law on the books for decades. Another is that Jerusalem was already the capital of Israel, and our formal recognition of that fact didn't make it any more so.

This was the point of a comment made by Menachem Begin, the first truly right-wing prime minister of Israel, just before his first visit with Margaret Thatcher, the British prime minister, in 1979. He was answering a question from the press: would he ask her to recognize Jerusalem as the capital of Israel? Begin and Thatcher were both conservative, after all, so it was expected that their interactions would be different from prior administrations. Begin responded, "I suppose if Prime Minister Thatcher asks me to recognize London as the capital of the United Kingdom I will do so, and then expect her to reciprocate by recognizing Jerusalem as the capital of Israel. You see, Jerusalem has been the capital of Israel for a thousand years longer than anyone has ever heard of the British Isles." In other words, an outside power's recognition doesn't make Jerusalem the capital of Israel any more than it already was.

The following day, I was able to accompany Governor and Mrs. Scott on a cultural visit to historic Jerusalem. It was pouring rain when I met them outside the gates of the Old City at 8:30 a.m. Jerusalem was deserted, partly because of the weather and partly because no one had been quite sure how residents would react to President Trump's announcement just twelve hours ago.

Through tears of joy I said, "Governor Scott, Mrs. Scott, for the past two thousand years, the Jewish people have been exiled from the land of Israel in a way that they were not in control of their own destiny. Even this year, when Israel celebrated its seventieth anniversary as the modern State of Israel, it was an incomplete celebration because it is the only country in the world for which the international community chooses to ignore the sovereign right of choosing its own capital. Last night, President Trump corrected a seventy-year wrong by America against our ally Israel. Right now, I am the first U.S. diplomat in history to have the honor and pleasure of welcoming you to Jerusalem, the capital of Israel."

The governor and I had a very firm handshake, and Mrs. Scott hugged me. The governor's head of security wiped away a tear, gave me a fist bump, and said, "Thank you for convincing us to be part of this historic moment."

We toured the Old City, visited the Western Wall, and then went to see the ancient City of David, an archeological site that I had not yet visited in my official capacity. I will describe it in more detail later, but first I want to focus on the Western Wall and how the protocol surrounding it encapsulates the obfuscation that was displayed by U.S. foreign policy more or less regardless of political party prior to President Trump.

In May 2017, after the president flew from Saudi Arabia directly to Israel, he became the first sitting U.S. president to visit the Western Wall. But he went there without any Israeli officials accompanying him. At that time, Jerusalem was the area of responsibility (AOR) for the U.S. Consulate located there, and the consul general stated clearly that Israeli officials had no right (according to U.S. policy) to accompany the president to the Western Wall. After all, in December 2016 the United States did not veto UN Resolution 2334, which essentially declared that every inch of land on the other side of the Green Line is occupied Palestinian land. Going to the Western Wall with an Israeli government official would be tantamount to recognizing Israeli rights to the wall, as opposed to enforcing our policy of shunning illegal occupiers. So President Trump, on his first and only visit to Israel, went to the Western Wall unaccompanied by Israeli officials. Even his official visit manifest recorded that he had visited Jerusalem but not necessarily Israel.

Consular staff also enforced a taboo against U.S. officials going to visit the City of David, a site that has great historical significance, but for that very reason it was regarded as controversial. The City of David is what many archeologists believe to have been the biblical city of King David. The site also includes the "Pilgrimage Road," the ancient street leading from the Pool of Siloam to the Temple of Solomon, which today runs beneath the East Jerusalem neighborhood of Silwan. The City of David is one of the most important archeological sites in the world. Its historical significance is obvious to anyone who visits, and to hundreds of millions of people it is also a place of holiness.

The archeological finds in the City of David provide clear evidence for the Jewish foundations of Jerusalem, yet the international community, through the United Nations and countless other well-funded NGOs, persistently denies this link. UNESCO, perhaps the most egregious of these organizations, has time and again chosen to delink Judaism from Jerusalem, in an effort to delegitimize Israel's rights to Jerusalem. There is a long game being played here, slowly degrading Israel's own confidence in its historical claims to the holy sites of Judaism, while making it uncomfortable for others to be supportive of Israel and its rights. Those playing this long game understand that this is a region where history is measured in centuries, and they expect to outlast any political pushback.

Up until 2017, they were winning. Recall that the United States abstained from the vote on UN Resolution 2334 rather than veto it in December 2016. The abstention gave credence to Israel's enemies and let them believe that if they tell a lie often enough and loud enough, it will eventually carry the day. If you give the enemies of truth and the enemies of our allies hope and oxygen, they will grow stronger, watching for the next opportunity to advance when America again shows moral weakness. It is actually well known that Jerusalem is deeply connected with Judaism, as well as Christianity and Islam. The willingness to wink and nod at the propagandists who deny it is more damaging to the United States than to Israel, because when our government compromises our own principles and decides that facts are inconvenient, we are the losers. The fiction could be seen for what it was, yet it was indulged and in some ways promoted by previous U.S. administrations, to the detriment of our allies and ourselves.

The denialism about Jerusalem derailed my first effort to visit the City of David. Soon after I arrived at the embassy, I was invited to visit the site by my dear friend Paul Packer, the chairman of the U.S. Presidential Commission to Preserve Heritage Abroad. Twice I worked with the City of David team and the U.S. Consulate in Jerusalem to scheduled a visit, only to be told that the U.S. Department of State did not permit visits to a site so controversial. In my naïveté, I didn't fully grasp why it would be controversial, so I asked for a briefing by the consulate staff. I was told in no uncertain terms that the City of David is a politically motivated archeological site, partly funded by the government of Israel, and that the project shows blatant disregard for the people living in the neighborhood, perhaps violating their human rights. This was a pretty strong accusation. I asked if the person briefing me had ever been to the site. I was told no, since doing so was discouraged for them as well. If a U.S. government official went to an archeological site funded by the Israeli government on the other side of the Green Line, it would be akin to recognizing Israel's right to be there, I was told, and that would be in violation of international law, UN Resolution 2334. I then asked how the State Department knew that the project was violating the rights of Silwan residents, and the answer was, "Many NGOs have reported to us about this." Since the U.S. government basically outsourced to NGOs the authority to determine when rights are being violated, there's an element of circular logic here.

Governors are not equally discouraged from visiting the City of David, however, because official U.S. government policy regulates the movements only of executive branch employees when they travel abroad. Members of Congress can set their own agendas, and their visits are supported but not dictated by the embassy or by administration policy. Governors traveling abroad do so on their own. Some liaise with the embassy, some do not. They are not obliged to follow administration policy either. I found it interesting that several governors had been to places in Judea and Samaria where members of previous administrations who were in charge of U.S. Middle East policy had never gone.

Since Governor Scott and Mrs. Scott were planning to visit the City of David while they were in Jerusalem in December, I figured it was the perfect time to break the taboo against executive officials going there. After the president's recognition of Jerusalem as the capital of Israel the evening before, my visiting an archeological site was not going to generate any additional news or backlash. I was enthralled by the riveting presentation of Zeev Orenstein, but walking on the very stones trod by the prophets, by Jesus, by saintly rabbis would have been thrilling enough in itself.

When I left the City of David that day, I was convinced that I needed to bring the ambassador to the site as soon as possible, and that it should become an American cultural heritage site under the patronage of the Commission to Preserve Heritage Abroad. Over the following three years, Friedman and I brought numerous cabinet secretaries to the City of David, including Steven Mnuchin, Mike Pompeo, Rick Perry, and Dan Brouillette, as well as two national security advisors, John Bolton and Robert O'Brien. On the night before the first-ever El Al flight from Israel to the UAE, which would bring action to the first Abraham Accords phone call, the entire peace team toured the City of David and the Western Wall. This was a special full-circle moment for me in my job at the embassy.

II

AS A MONK IN SOLITUDE

Mike Pence's first trip to Israel as vice president, in January 2018, was the highest-level visit since I had arrived at the embassy. My relationship with Orit and Edna, plus my friendship with key members of Pence's team, gave me the ability to serve as the go-between for all parties involved in making sure the visit would be optimal. On this visit, Pence became the first vice president to address the Knesset. This was an extraordinary moment, especially as it came directly on the heels of the Jerusalem recognition. The people of Israel knew the Trump administration was different from previous administrations, and inviting the vice president to address the Knesset was just one of the historic honors they gave him.

When the speech concluded, the vice president's team and the embassy team supporting the visit got into the motorcade and returned to the King David Hotel. This was the hotel of choice for many of the senior visits during the Trump administration, and its lobby and patio served as my Jerusalem-based meeting spot before the opening of the embassy in the city. Ambassador Friedman invited a small group including members of Pence's team and Netanyahu's team for a celebratory dinner, and I was lucky enough to be invited too.

We ate in the private room downstairs, and there was hardly enough space around the table for the waiters and the security guards to maneuver. Everyone ordered steak except for Yoav Horowitz, Netanyahu's chief of staff. He ordered fish, and he took some good-natured ribbing for it. A quiet guy and well respected by all of us, he had not spoken much up to that point. He turned to me and said, "Do you know why I ordered the fish?"

"Nope. Why?"

"It teaches me a lesson when I order fish. I am reminded why the fish wound up on the plate."

There was a dramatic pause as the other thirteen people in the room all looked at Yoav, awaiting the punchline.

"The fish," he continued, "wound up on the plate because it opened its mouth when it shouldn't have."

That line still resonates with me several years later, as I believe it probably does with everyone else who was in the room that evening. Much of what was accomplished in the U.S.-Israel relationship leading up to the Abraham Accords came about because a small, select team knew enough to listen more than talk, and when there was something to say, we knew whom to say it to and when.

Later that evening, Ambassador Dermer asked Friedman, "What is it that Lightstone does all day?"

"I am not really sure," David replied. "When I need him he is there, and when I don't need him he is also there. But the way I have pictured him in the last ninety days is as a monk in solitude by candlelight going through every piece of paper that has ever been written by the State Department, and, more importantly, every piece of paper that will be written by the State Department, crossing out 'illegally occupied' and replacing it with 'disputed.'"

Everyone had a nice chuckle. The systematic changes to the State Department reports had just emerged in the news, causing angst among the peace processors and their associated NGOs and preferred media outlets. The people at this dinner, on the other hand, were greatly pleased to see the reports catching up so quickly (if not fully) with the Trump administration's policies, especially because there was no love lost for the secretary of state at the time, Rex Tillerson.

Vice President Pence had worked with Ambassador Friedman toward the goal of recognizing Jerusalem as the capital of Israel, and now they had two days to share the experience of a vastly improved U.S.-Israel relationship. My own relationship with the vice president also became stronger from this visit, and I worked together with his team on numerous exciting projects. When it comes to the U.S.-Israel relationship, Pence has a famous catchphrase: "If the world knows nothing else, let it know this. America stands with Israel."

12

"NICE SOCKS"

——————

Bill Haslem, former governor of Tennessee, was in Israel on a personal trip in the spring of 2018 and he wanted to reconnect with Benjamin Netanyahu, as they had developed a meaningful relationship. I received a phone call from the Prime Minister's Office saying that Netanyahu had forty-five minutes to meet with Haslem and asking if Ambassador Friedman could join them. I called David, who was then in Herzliya Pituach, at least seventy-five minutes away. He said I should go to the meeting in his stead, so I informed the Prime Minister's Office that I would be coming and then promptly headed out.

Luckily I was wearing a suit, even though it was a Sunday. Unfortunately, as I realized en route, I was wearing socks from my casual Sunday series, which included a Dr. Seuss collection. That day I had chosen bright yellow one fish two fish red fish blue fish socks. I scrambled around in my car for a backup pair, but alas, I had none with me. Still, I wasn't too worried, since every meeting I had been in with the prime minister up to then had been in the official meeting room, where we sat around a large table, so the odds of anyone noticing my socks seemed pretty low.

I arrived at the Prime Minister's Office five minutes before Governor Haslem and his son, so I was able to welcome them. While we didn't know each other, we had a lot of acquaintances in common, and we had a great conversation for about half an hour in the waiting room. I apologized that Friedman couldn't make it on such short notice, and Haslem said not to worry, it was just a courtesy call. We discussed current events in the Middle East and the Trump policies toward Israel. Four or five people from the office came up to say hello and asked me to introduce them to Haslem. It made me look like a well-connected official, and I felt pretty good about myself.

When Netanyahu's chief of staff, Yoav Horowitz, announced that the prime minister was ready to meet, I jumped up and headed toward the main conference room. I moved too quickly. Yoav ushered the three of us into the prime minister's personal office. This was my first time walking into that office, and I was equal parts giddy and nervous. There were five comfortable chairs and no table. Netanyahu's foreign policy advisor, Reuven Azar, was also there. We all remained standing as Netanyahu prepared his pipe, filling the room with a delicious aroma, if you ask me. Then we sat down in the comfortable chairs, and I crossed my right leg over my left at a right angle, as I normally do. Suddenly the most conspicuous object in the room was my bright yellow Dr. Seuss socks, one fish two fish red fish blue fish. I will never forget the prime minister looking at my socks, looking at me, and then moving his lips slightly. To this day, I tell myself it was a suppressed grin, though I am pretty sure it was a scowl.

During the conversation, Haslem mentioned "Lightstone" several times in making a point, and it became evident that Netanyahu wasn't sure who was being referenced. At the end, he finally asked who this "Lightstone" was. Then Haslem wondered if he had gotten my name wrong. Reuven Azar visibly suppressed a giggle as he pointed to me, and I was embarrassed all over again.

When we walked out of the office, Netanyahu patted me on the back and said, "Nice socks."

The prime minister would get to know me a lot better in the next few years. As I've mentioned, my position at the embassy didn't really exist in foreign ministry protocol, so until I proved my worth and made my own connections, I was frequently in a somewhat awkward situation. That changed once I had experience dealing with various offices, sometimes working closely with the people in charge.

At official Israeli events, Ambassador Friedman would have the seat of greatest honor, normally next to the prime minister, the president, or the Speaker of the Knesset, and I would be seated next to him. After me came the ambassadors from other important allied countries. While this seating arrangement was directly against protocol in an arena where protocol is highly important, it conveyed two important messages. From Israel to the United States: You are our most important ally, now and hopefully always. To the rest of the world: You are all interested in peace in the Middle East, and the only trusted broker is the United States. All paths toward peace must run through American leadership.

Let me say again that David Friedman was not a typical ambassador. Through his relationship with Trump, Kushner, Pence, and later Pompeo, he was the top U.S. policymaker in the region. I was the guy lucky enough to work alongside him for four years, acting as his gatekeeper and following up on all things that mattered to him. For that reason, I was placed next to him at nearly every important event and meeting.

Israel's love of America and its dependence on the United States are pretty much an unquestioned foundation of Israeli foreign policy, but it isn't just a one-way street. Netanyahu had a phrase I heard in person more than a hundred times: "Israel has no greater friend than the United States and the United States has no greater friend than Israel." He uttered it again and again when he had precious moments to spend with the most senior leadership of the United States. This message was not like the tongue-in-cheek T-shirt you can purchase at most AIPAC conventions saying: "Don't worry America, Israel has your back." While some of the formal institutions of the U.S. government preferred a lukewarm relationship with Israel, the Trump administration from top to bottom treated Israel as its number one ally in the region, and possibly in the world. There was no doubt about which country will be with America when the chips are down. Clearly Israel will be there to help in any way it can. That is one reason why it simply made sense to put our embassy in Israel's capital.

13

HERE TO STAY

The State Department was warned by its embassy contacts far and wide that the world would blow up if President Trump recognized Jerusalem as the capital of Israel. He recognized Jerusalem, and the world did not blow up. He was then told by the State Department and other D.C. institutions that the explosion would happen when the embassy building was constructed in Jerusalem, but he knew this was fearmongering of the worst kind. He trusted his man on the ground, David Friedman, and if David said it would be okay, it would be. He also checked with Jared Kushner on what Arab and Muslim countries would think about the move. Most of them realized that they should not be on the other side of the United States when it fulfilled its own law on the books for over two decades. They were not rooting for this decision but knew they shouldn't be standing in the way.

Secretary Tillerson was not in favor of the Jerusalem announcement, and it seemed as though he would do everything in his power to deny the president and the ambassador the opportunity to open the embassy in their first term, if at all. But our embassy team was abuzz with excitement from the moment President Trump announced that he was instructing Ambassador Friedman to commence the process of moving the embassy from Tel Aviv to Jerusalem. The United States opens new embassies around the world from time to time, and usually it does not gain much publicity outside the host country. But all things related to Israel get an enormous amount of attention, so it was clear that this embassy opening was not going to go under the radar.

Normally the process takes years, and I thought there could be an advantage in not moving too quickly to the opening. I formulated a plan for getting the most bang for the embassy opening buck, with a timeline allowing six months for site selection, another six months for the plans to be revealed, then six months before a big logo reveal, and finally fifteen months more until the formal opening. In September 2020, two months before the election, the president would come to Jerusalem for a huge ceremony during which he would place the cornerstone. I was very pleased with this plan. After all, I had come into my position with more of a political history than David Friedman.

With paper in hand, I went to the ambassador's home in Herzliya on December 8 at around 10 a.m., hoping I was there early enough to be offered an omelet for breakfast. Luck was on my side that day. I joined David in his study, and he settled into his big easy chair while I sat in my traditional place on a two-seater couch to his right. The residence staff, who always treated us like family, came in with an omelet and coffee for me, and coffee with an abundance of milk for the ambassador.

After some small talk, I began laying out my plan for the embassy opening. I may have gotten thirty seconds into my pitch when David put his coffee down and placed his phone on the table in front of his chair. I knew that something was wrong, and I figured maybe he hadn't heard me clearly, so I tried to start from the beginning again. I said that the president needed to view this as a political gift that keeps on giving. Every visit from a high-ranking visitor would play a role in the eventual opening of the embassy, and over time there would be a steady accumulation of good news, which would be essential for the midterm elections and eventually the presidential election. David allowed me to get through the entire plan this time, but he still didn't seem too pleased by it.

As soon as he began to speak, I realized that I had looked at the matter through the wrong lens. He noted how improbable it was for either of us to be sitting where we were, and he explained that if the bureaucracy was going to view us as summer interns, we needed to value each day and every opportunity it brought. He appreciated the effort I had put into mapping out a schedule that would be convenient for politics, but he was emphatic that what we do representing the United States of America in Israel must transcend politics if it is to endure. He told me to rip up the schedule and write a new one. I asked what he wanted me to write on it, and he replied: "Do the right thing as soon as it is possible to get it done, never later than that." Those words are firmly implanted in my mind and written on a piece of paper on my desk. Those words became my guideline for seizing the opportunities ahead.

I brought another piece of paper to David's home that day, and this one came from my seven-year-old daughter, Shayna. The move to Israel had been a great challenge for my wife and four little children, who needed to adjust to a new country, a new home, new schools, and a new language. I tried to bring purpose and meaning to their experience by involving them in the exciting parts of my position as much as possible. David and Tammy Friedman were incredibly gracious and accommodating, not just allowing but encouraging their participation. For the recognition of Jerusalem as the capital of Israel, I asked Shayna to do an artistic rendering of what the new embassy should look like. She stayed up all night drawing and redrawing until she was satisfied with her blueprint. I presented it to David, thinking he would get a kick out of it. He was delighted, and he added his signature. Then I hung the drawing in my office in Tel Aviv.

One month later I received a note directing me to speak with our chief security officer. That is never a good thing. I went down to his office, wondering what this could be about. He sat me down and explained that I had violated embassy security protocols. Confused, I asked for clarification. Apparently the regional security officers were none too pleased with Shayna's drawing of the future embassy in Jerusalem, maintaining that it showed classified spaces! They informed me that they took the drawing and had it destroyed in the same way that classified documents are destroyed. I didn't know whether to laugh or cry. Shayna's drawing of an embassy looked very much how you would expect from a seven-year-old, complete with a unicorn.

I am sure that I wasn't the only person who drew up a politically advantageous schedule for the embassy opening. I am sure that someone at or near the White House wished to turn this into a political spectacle, but the president's direction was the same as the ambassador's: I promised to get it done, so get it done as soon as possible and as correctly as possible. Acting quickly would demonstrate the principle: If you say something, mean something. And the message would be heard by both friends and adversaries across the world.

I am also sure that most of the countries in the region assumed that the recognition of Jerusalem as the capital of Israel was pure political theater. After all, U.S. embassies usually take between five and fifteen years to build, and much can change in the meantime. Normally a research committee is formed, and it reports its findings to the State Department, which then puts out a request for information (RFI), and on that basis the State Department puts out a request for proposal (RFP), which is reviewed by the original committee (by now possibly consisting of different people), and then a tender evaluation committee reviews bids, after which there is a legal review, and finally construction can begin. As you can see, the red tape can take an awfully long time to unwind. For the record, I am not against that sort of process in all cases. While it slows things down, it does help keep the government honest and keep actions in line with goals. Yet there are times when the United States needs to act like the one true superpower and assert itself with alacrity.

Throughout the Middle East, with the exception of Israel, when a decision is made by a leader, it does not go through a long committee process before action is taken. Action speaks volumes louder than words in this region. This is why Ambassador Friedman initiated a greatly expedited process, and President Trump backed it with the full weight of the White House. The embassy in Jerusalem would be built and opened within a time frame that no one in or out of the U.S. government would have expected, and at a fraction of the anticipated budget. At his rallies, the president told the raucous crowds that his State Department (i.e., Rex Tillerson) tried to make him agree to a ten-year rollout costing over $1.5 billion, but his man on the ground, David Friedman, figured out how to get it done in just over six months and for less than $1 million.

This does not mean the process was conducted in the manner of a Middle Eastern autocracy. The U.S. government has an enormous bureaucracy that can hobble even the best initiatives with red tape. President Trump and his team were determined to find the best possible way to execute the plan on behalf of the American people, and believed they were better positioned to make those decisions than an unelected, unaccountable bureaucratic class.

Israel would probably have liked a more drawn-out process to use as an opportunity to persuade other countries to move their embassies and to gather more bipartisan support in the United States. The cottage industry of peace processors urged the United States to extract concessions from Israel in return, which missed the entire point of the embassy opening, especially in such a short time frame. The speed of the opening demonstrated to Washington that when there is a will, government projects can be done better and more efficiently than they are usually done. It also sent a message to the leaders of other countries throughout the world, especially in the Middle East, but also Russia, China, and Iran: The United States would not only make bold statements, but follow those statements with action, and do so unapologetically. It helped create a foreign policy trend of action consistent with the principles of standing with our allies and not yielding an inch to adversaries.

The U.S. Embassy in Jerusalem was officially opened on May 14, 2018, at 4:11 p.m. It was seventy years to the minute after President Harry Truman—against the advice of his secretary of state—recognized Israel as a state, which in turn was eleven minutes after Israel became a state, on May 14, 1948, at 4:00 p.m. local time. The embassy opening was one of the largest, most important diplomatic events of my lifetime, as well as one of the greatest days of my life. I was blessed that Ambassador Friedman included my family as guests.

David and I coordinated all the events that surrounded the official opening ceremony without additional embassy support. This was a daunting task, as there was a very large delegation coming from the White House, including Steven Mnuchin, Jared Kushner and Ivanka Trump, Avi Berkowitz, and many more. Governor Rick Scott was attending, and there was a delegation from Congress, as well as informal delegations that came to

Israel for the occasion. The guest list included supporters of the U.S.-Israel relationship, plus a Who's Who of Israeli government officials and nongovernmental leaders. This was the most coveted invitation in Israel in decades, if not ever. The embassy team did an amazing job of orchestrating the most watched U.S. embassy opening in history. Besides the official ceremony, there were various side events for the hundreds of visitors to Jerusalem who were not federal employees. Hosting events for Americans is not in the embassy's purview, so it was up to Friedman and me to coordinate these events.

Because of security concerns, all guests met at Teddy Stadium in Jerusalem to be cleared, and then boarded buses to the embassy. Andrew, an embassy officer who was in charge of the check-in and bus departure terminal, had the logistics down to a science. Many of the attendees had not been on a bus since elementary school. Andrew told me a fascinating story: About thirty people waiting for a bus were informed that it would be seven minutes until the next one arrived. In the meantime, they took the mandatory selfies, but also wanted to make those seven minutes as meaningful as they could. It was an eclectic group—evangelicals, rabbis, financial supporters of the president, leaders of organizations that champion the U.S.-Israel relationship. Michele Bachmann seized the moment and led the crowd in songs that were familiar to all, from English hymns, to "Hava Nagila," a Jewish folksong, and "Hatikvah," the Israeli national anthem, and concluding with "God Bless America" as the bus arrived. Andrew remarked to me how uplifting it was to see some very important people view this event as a time for spiritual growth as well as witnessing history.

Pastor John Hagee gave the benediction at the end of the opening ceremony, and his words captured the policy imperative as well as the spiritual power of the moment. His theme was that the United States was sending an unambiguous message to the world that Jerusalem lives and is the eternal capital of Israel. In his booming voice, he said: "Let them hear it in Tehran, Jerusalem lives. Let the Hezbollah terrorists understand that Jerusalem lives. Let Hamas know that Jerusalem lives. Let Ramallah know that Jerusalem lives. Let Washington know that Jerusalem lives." The United States as the unquestioned superpower of the world was building its embassy in Jerusalem. Despite all the criticism, it was going to stand by Israel, a Jewish democratic state, whose capital, Jerusalem, would forever be linked to its Jewish foundations.

The fulfillment of the 1995 law challenged the notion that Israel was a temporary aberration in the Middle East, a blip in history. It had arrived on the scene through colonial machinations, the thinking went, so it would disappear into the annals of history as yet another mistaken adventure in the Middle East. But when the world's undisputed superpower puts its embassy in Israel's capital, then Israel is no longer a mistake or a blip in history. It is here to stay. Now the rest of the world needs to reckon with this fact. The message was certainly heard in Abu Dhabi, the capital of the United Arab Emirates, and in Manama, the capital of Bahrain.

In a keynote speech, Jared Kushner said that peace was now closer than it had been the day before. This was widely ridiculed as a trite throwaway line. In the following days, newspapers in the United States and across Europe juxtaposed pictures of Jared and Ivanka at the embassy in Jerusalem with images of smoke, fire, and blood at the border of Gaza, more than fifty miles away, where Palestinians had launched violent protests, and dozens were killed as a result. The purpose of the split screens was to convey the idea of causation, suggesting that the opening of the embassy led to the death of "innocent" young Palestinians. Anyone who followed the region with any attention to detail knew this was disingenuous, because while there was a connection between the events, those killed were not innocent. But for the uninformed, it was like fish food to the sharks, portraying Jared and Ivanka as callous and uncaring. Media reports conveyed poorly concealed glee at the death of Palestinians if it could be blamed on Jared and Ivanka, and by extension Donald Trump. Even worse, by implying that the protests were justified, the media coverage was essentially rooting for violence and mayhem, which would then reinforce the Palestinian veto on U.S. policy. Perversely, Hamas knew that people it sent to rush the fence would be killed and that the resulting split-screen image would be broadly welcomed by the mainstream press. The entire episode was scripted for the sake of media coverage. Much of the media on the ground knew this was happening, yet everyone played along with the script.

Within two days, over 95 percent of the "victims" at the Gaza border were identified as terrorists who had been trying to enter Israel to commit acts of violence. This was not difficult to predict, but it didn't fit the desired narrative. Corrections and retractions were made, but hardly anyone ever reads such corrections, and meanwhile people have made judgments and decisions.

On May 15, we went to work in the embassy just opened the previous day. I was immediately flooded with email requests to meet there. Simply being at the embassy was a thrill for many people who support a strong U.S.-Israel relationship. Israeli government officials, tourists, and groups from around the world wanted to visit the embassy. David Friedman, already the most influential ambassador to Israel in history by a long shot, became the most important person to meet in Israel aside from the prime minister.

The embassy relocation was an enormous win for the United States, and for our allies. First, the president executed on a campaign promise, which was actually to apply the law of the land. From a policy perspective, this removed an enormous amount of vagary in the U.S.-Israel relationship. As long as the United States didn't recognize Israel's right to choose its own capital, the relationship would not be complete. Allies can and do have many issues on which they do not see eye to eye, but the location of an ally's capital would normally not be such an issue. Moreover, it was not an issue in the actual law of the United States, but out-siders were allowed to exercise a veto on that law, which created imbalance in the relationship. When the Jerusalem Embassy Act was finally put into effect, the external veto on U.S. policy was ended. The message sent to the world was that the United States would take itself seriously, and stand with its allies proactively. Hezbollah, Hamas, and the Palestinian Authority were put on notice. Iran and North Korea were put on notice.

While this action strengthened the United States in the Middle East and beyond, I believe that more could have been accom-plished if the secretary of state until April 2018 had been working for the president instead of against him, at least in the U.S.-Israel relationship. Rex Tillerson managed to take one of the boldest and most morally just diplomatic decisions by a U.S. administration in decades and blunt its usefulness. In numerous conversations with policymakers from allied nations, I was informed that Secretary Tillerson never once asked them to follow the United States' lead in recognizing Jerusalem and moving their embas-sies. Many countries got the distinct impression that this was not the policy of the United States, but only the policy of Donald Trump. Guatemala and Paraguay opened embassies in Jerusalem just a few days after the United States did. While I cannot prove it, I believe that had Mike Pompeo been the secretary of state between Decembers 6, 2017, and May 14, 2018, there would have been twenty more embassies moved to Jerusalem. And if moving the U.S. Embassy to Jerusalem brought peace closer to the region, then all those additional embassies in Jerusalem would have brought peace faster and more comprehensively.

The vast majority of my embassy colleagues in fact worked diligently and professionally alongside me and Ambassador Friedman. They may have agreed, they may have disagreed. Some of them shared their opinions with me, and others did not. But a few people tried everything in their power to disrupt the policy agenda of the president. A few embassy employees would schedule planning meetings when the ambassador and I were out on government-to-government meetings, or even change the location of the meeting when I was already in a skiff (a room without any electronics). By the time I realized that the meeting was in another room, it was already in progress, and it is bad form to walk into a skiff after the scheduled start time of a meeting.

Small acts of insubordination as well as poor decision making by a secretary of state hampered the effectiveness of the Trump administration and damaged the honor of the United States. Such actions confused the messaging when clarity and consistency were needed. If you are a government official or employee, you are not obliged to agree with the policies of an administration, and in fact it would be weird if anyone fully agreed with someone else. But once a decision is made, you can either support it, or ask for a different assignment, or resign, but you cannot continue to do the job you were hired to do while working against the decisions of the elected official who sets policy. Doing so demonstrates a lack of moral courage.

Recall that the Senate passed a resolution 90-0 reaffirming the Jerusalem Embassy Act in June 2017. At the time, there were not many issues that got the same level of bipartisan agreement in the Senate. But eleven months later, not a single congressional Democrat showed up to the embassy opening.

While this was a coveted ticket for Israelis and supporters of the U.S.-Israel relationship, the opening of the embassy was the fulfillment of U.S. law, and every member of Congress who wished to attend would have been welcomed warmly as an honored guest. Afterward, six Democratic members of Congress published an open letter saying that they were not invited, and reporters then called to ask Ambassador Friedman why he had not invited them. Yet all of the legislators who signed the letter had in fact been invited. They got blowback from constituents for not attending, which is why they published the letter, assuming that Friedman would roll over and ignore the complaint. He didn't, and neither did the Republican members who came to the opening ceremony. They said on the record that they had personally invited members of both parties.

During the four years I was at the embassy, dozens of congressional delegations visited Israel, and none of them, including the delegation to the embassy opening, came at the invitation of the embassy in Israel. Members of Congress know full well how to come to Israel, and our embassy was under strict instructions from the day Friedman arrived to treat every delegation with the utmost professionalism. I am pleased to say that we did so.

I would like to say I was surprised by the partisan response from Congress, but I had become quite jaded during David Friedman's Senate confirmation process. One particular Democratic senator's position was typical, though he stated it more clearly than others. David and I were in a closed-door meeting with this senator and a prominent longtime supporter of his who had made no secret of the fact that his support was based upon the senator's commitment to the U.S.-Israel relationship. Friedman talked about his policies and his hope that the relationship would be above partisan politics, and said that a broad bipartisan vote in favor of his confirmation would serve that end. After all, just a few years earlier, President Obama's choice for ambassador, Dan Shapiro, was approved by a voice vote; it was a foregone conclusion that he would be approved, so a more formal vote was unnecessary. This senator replied, in essence: "One of us can do something about the bipartisan support for Israel, and it is you. Decline your nomination and tell your friend the president to pick someone who will be more evenhanded with the Israelis and the Palestinians." A few months later, this senator was among the ninety who voted for the Jerusalem Embassy Act resolution. The hypocrisy was nauseating.

14

THE DISASTER
DID NOT HAPPEN

The Republican and Democratic parties have become increasingly polarized on many issues, which is unfortunate since many of the challenges facing the United States would be better addressed with bipartisan consensus. The widening gulf is most obvious on domestic issues but extends to foreign policy as well, and particularly to U.S.-Israel policy. The difference can be understood in terms of idealism versus realism. Looking at Israel and its neighbors, Democrats tend to see great inequality, which is not ideal, and so they believe that the United States must act to balance things out. Progressives view our relationship with Israel at least partially through the lens of the Palestinian conflict and the supposed human rights violations perpetrated by Israel. For these reasons, Democrats believe there should be daylight between the United States and Israel. To conservative politicians, looking through a lens of realism, Israel represents making the most of a challenging situation. As Senator Lindsey Graham is fond of saying, "Israel has the nicest house in a pretty rough neighborhood." Conservatives have found a staunch ally in Israel not just because of shared values, but also for practical reasons, from economic opportunity to life-and-death intelligence and defense cooperation. The Republican Party therefore favors strengthening the U.S.-Israel relationship. Republicans also want to offer the Palestinians and others in the region an opportunity for a close relationship, but only if they earn it.

There are some who believe that bipartisanship in U.S. policy toward Israel is more important than strong support for Israel, and who claim that bipartisan support is the best thing for Israel in the long run. If Democrats cannot be moved away from their line on the Palestinian conflict, in this thinking, then it is best to make sure the Republicans don't go too far in support of Israel, because that would prevent Democratic support. This rather lopsided argument arises from the principle of equity between Israel and the Palestinians, which in the progressive view requires decreasing support for Israel. Pursuing equity in the name of bipartisanship would damage the U.S.-Israel relationship, which in turn would be harmful to U.S. interests.

There is no equivalency between what Israel and Palestinians contribute to the United States. Because of our special relationship, the United States has been a chief beneficiary of Israeli technological breakthroughs, making the relationship a valuable asset in the global competition for technological supremacy. Downgrading that relationship would thus be harmful to the United States. Second, Israel is a democratic state that strives for excellence and shares core values with Americans. The Palestinians have not demonstrated commitment to those values or pursued achievement in anywhere near the same measure. Instead, they are mired in their denialism. If they maintain this posture and the United States grants them equal importance with Israel, it will reduce our moral authority and influence around the world, as well as the faith our allies have in us.

Let me be clear that it is far better for the United States to have more allies and friends rather than fewer. If too close an alignment with one country will jeopardize friendship with other countries, especially ones that are of strategic importance, the U.S. government must do what is in the best interest of the United States, not any other country. Even so, the notion that being close with Israel is dangerous to our other relationships throughout the world arises from faulty thinking.

The first error is the belief that we are stronger as a nation when we don't play favorites but appreciate everyone equally. Or if we do play favorites, we must always root for the little guy, for the sake of equity. This type of wrongheaded thinking brought us the renaming of terrorists as freedom fighters, and the insistence that the Palestinians must get endless indulgence, while Israel must be penalized for its success. But in fact, some countries are more important to the United States than others, because they have more values and interests in common with us, and because their friendship provides us more benefit.

The reason we support Israel is not because it needs our financial and diplomatic assistance to survive. Israel is not a delicate flower that would not exist without constant charity. It is a regional superpower, an international tech powerhouse, and a country with robust human rights, civil rights, and economic freedom. It is a beacon of light in a difficult neighborhood. Israel defends itself by itself, and it is often a target of attack by those who wish harm to the United States as well. It serves as a forward base for U.S. interests, providing us with intelligence and tactics, and sometimes taking actions on our behalf that we cannot or will not take ourselves. We support Israel because doing so is in our national interest.

Another error in thinking about the alliance begins with the way that information is gathered by diplomats in a typical career.

Embassies around the world post well-trained individuals who spend a large part of their professional lives working to further the goals of the United States abroad. While I don't agree with all of them, and in fact I may disagree with most of them, nearly every person I had the privilege of working with was a stellar professional. But regardless of how well qualified and ambitious they are, the system has some inherent flaws that produce an echo chamber of misleading information.

Let's look specifically at the Middle East, although I am sure that a similar problem affects many other embassies and therefore U.S. foreign policy decisions in other regions. Foreign service officers move around every three years to a different post, but most often within the same region. If you work in the Middle East, you may have five postings in Muslim/Arab countries, where you will connect with key embassy contacts. Since you are in country for only three years, you are likely to inherit your initial contacts (if not all of them) from the person you are replacing. Governments and other organizations understand the value of these contacts for themselves, and they actively work to ensure that U.S. Embassy officers have warm and strong connections with people who will deliver the desired message. In nondemocratic countries, even not-for-profit organizations need the government's blessing to operate and exert influence, so they are likely to send a government-approved message.

It is the job of U.S. foreign service officers to promote the interests of the United States in every posting. To that end, they network with their contacts and discuss what would enhance relations between the United States and the country to which they are posted. In Muslim/Arab countries, the message would invariably be: "If only you distanced yourself from Israel and showed more favor to the downtrodden Palestinians, we would be closer to the United States. And when the Palestinian issue is resolved, all other issues in the Middle East will go away." Of course, the message is conveyed with more nuance, but it will be repeated again and again in various Middle East postings. One officer may hear it countless times for fifteen years in five different countries.

Now, suppose that the hypothetical officer still has two more postings, both of them in Israel: one at the embassy in Tel Aviv and the other at the consulate in Jerusalem. Not-for-profits have full freedom of operation in Israel, so embassy contacts are not obliged to deliver a government-approved message. Instead, almost all U.S. Embassy contacts in Israel, and especially in Jerusalem, reinforce the notion that Israel is the problem and that strengthening ties with Palestinians is the solution.

Multiply that one diplomat's experience by all the other U.S. diplomats in the region, and you can see what will be the dominant message sent back to the State Department from embassies in the Middle East. Cable after cable will convey the idea that the cause of all problems in the Middle East lies in Israel's occupation of Palestine. Peace will blossom if only the United States distances itself from Israel and shows more favor to the Palestinians. By sheer volume, that message has overwhelmed a commonsense view of realities on the ground.

It illustrates a simple truth that I learned when I studied accounting as a university freshman: Crap in equals crap out. Pardon the crassness, but the lesson has stuck with me for more than twenty years. An accountant cannot produce high-quality reports without sound data. Unverifiable or faulty data can only result in bad reports, where incorrect information is covered with a veneer of professionalism. Unfortunately, much of U.S. foreign policy has rested on reports that begin with bad data, and not because the people who write the reports are incompetent. I believe that reasonable people at every stage of the data-in process are willing to question it, but the echo chamber that reinforces those ideas is too powerful for any one individual to overcome. The resulting groupthink has caused enormous damage to the success of the United States internationally and in the Middle East specifically.

What's more, our traditional friends and allies gather information the same way. Our embassy personnel tend to hang out socially with embassy personnel from allied nations. They share what they have learned from their contacts. In fact, most U.S. Embassy contacts are also contacts for the French, the British, the Canadians, and so on, not just in Israel but at nearly every diplomatic posting throughout the Middle East. The echo chamber is international.

This is why nearly every professional in the State Department pushed back against the president's recognition of Jerusalem as the capital of Israel, and later against the opening of the embassy in Jerusalem. This is why nearly every one of our allies called the president and recommended against both of those actions. All of their combined data told them that these would be catastrophic moves, sending shockwaves from Malaysia to Morocco. Everyone ran around like their hair was on fire and tried every method in their arsenal to prevent these decisions from being actualized.

When the disaster did not happen, there was no discernible reflection about how all the professionals could have been so wrong. There wasn't a meeting with our allies to consider what else we might be wrong about. There should have been an explosion, but there wasn't. The professionals couldn't be wrong, so it was assumed that the summer interns were lucky.

We know why the establishment was wrong about the embassy in Jerusalem. Crap in equals crap out. We need to challenge our diplomatic system to set up a process for evaluating the quality of the information that comes in. The foreign service officers are bright, motivated, and more than capable of assessing the information provided to the embassy and setting up guardrails against NGOs dictating our foreign policy.

15

DEFUNDING HATE

———————

There are many reasons for the United States to give strong support to Israel, but that does not mean being against the Palestinian people, because Israel is not the cause of Palestinian problems. In fact, no one has done more harm to the Palestinian people than their current leadership, whether it is Hamas in Gaza or the Palestinian Authority in the West Bank. Their main leadership technique is blaming Israel for every ill that befalls their people, thus abdicating their own responsibility. When world leaders, international organizations, or members of Congress allow this blame shifting, the Palestinian people suffer.

The Palestinian leaders have been more intent on destroying Israel than on helping their own people. Although the Palestinian Authority is considered the moderate peace partner (by comparison with Hamas), it offers a financial incentive for the murder of Jews in terrorist acts. The more Jews killed, the bigger the reward to the families of terrorists who die during the attack. In order to hold the PA accountable for this outrage, Congress passed the Taylor Force Act in December 2017. The bill was named in memory of a U.S. Army veteran and West Point graduate who was studying in Israel on a special program with Vanderbilt

University when he was stabbed to death in a terrorist attack that also wounded ten other people on March 8, 2016. Since the terrorist was then neutralized by Israeli security, the Palestinian Authority gave the terrorist's family a monthly stipend several times what an average person earns in the Palestinian territories. Once the bill became law, the U.S. government could not give money directly to the Palestinian Authority as long as the "pay to slay" policy continued. The PA could easily solve the self-made economic problem that resulted, but chooses instead to maintain its policy out of a warped sense of principle.

There are other ways that the Palestinian leaders elevate enmity toward Jews over the well-being of the Palestinian people. One involves the United Nations Relief and Works Agency (UNRWA) and the schools it sponsors in the Palestinian territories. For decades it has been clear that UNRWA schools perpetuate the Israeli-Palestinian conflict by teaching hatred. Here is a typical math question from the UNRWA school curriculum: "If one martyr blows up a bus and kills seven Zionists, how many martyrs does it take to kill 28 Zionists?" This is one of the most insidious forms of hatred, injected into a subject that should be objective, and then fed into young children's minds at every opportunity. It makes hatred second nature to Palestinian kids.

What's worse, this educational content is acceptable to UNRWA and its supporters. Donors, which are primarily national governments, did not demand hate-free education in the Palestinian territories. I remember my first meeting with the embassy professionals in charge of the United States' relationship with UNRWA. They knew that I was against funding UNRWA, so they gave a presentation explaining that the organization, with their help, had reduced the educational content imbued with hatred and anti-Semitism from 13 percent to 8 percent. The situation was "getting better," I was assured by a staff member.

"How can we justify putting a single dollar more into this type of education?" I asked her.

She quickly pivoted, realizing that I was not impressed with a reduction in anti-Semitism in the UNRWA curriculum, and pointed out that the United States no longer funds curriculum development; it only funds teacher training and salaries.

"So that means we teach teachers how to better teach their curriculum?" I asked.

"Yes."

I was infuriated. The implicit assumption of my colleague was that we could not expect the Palestinians to stop hating the Israelis or to stop teaching hatred to their children. All we could hope for was a little bit less hatred. It reminded me of a terrible joke: "Q: What do you call an anti-Semite? A: Someone who hates Jews more than you should."

Why do we have such low expectations of the Palestinians? Teaching children to hate is inexcusable. It perpetuates conflict. So why do donors and policymakers indulge it? Imagine if those schools were used to promote peace and tolerance. I'm not saying that it would quickly produce a large group of Palestinian leaders ready to make challenging compromises for the sake of peace, but a change in education would certainly increase the odds that such leaders emerge.

Our ambassador to the United Nations, Nikki Haley, addressed the issue in a speech at the United Nations on July 24, 2108. She explained how UNRWA not only doesn't help, but actually does harm, and therefore the United States would no longer be party to it. She underscored that we as a nation are open to new solutions, but not to policies that foster bigotry. It was a masterful speech, and many found it refreshing to hear a politico speak truth so frankly.

It was greatly satisfying to hear, at the end of August, that the

United States had finally chosen to halt funding for UNRWA. The announcement prompted an international game of chicken. On the one hand, there was the not-very-subtle threat from some countries that unrest would be inevitable without UNRWA, and that people—meaning Israelis and Americans—would die. On the other hand, many of the countries making this threat pledged money to replace the withdrawn U.S. funding. Yet almost no cash ended up coming in from those countries. They paid lip service to the need for UNRWA, but preferred to see the American taxpayers footing the bill.

In Ambassador Haley's office several weeks later, I was surprised to hear a few members of the Trump administration ask her opinion on restarting UNRWA funding for one more year. They suggested that the withdrawal of funds might set off the next intifada. After all, the UNRWA schools did provide some education, so it would be kids who suffered from the defunding. Ideas were thrown around the room rather half-heartedly. There seemed to be a feeling that the conversation needed to be had, even if everyone knew what the correct answer was.

Finally, Nikki threw down the gauntlet. "If you choose to restart funding to UNRWA," she boomed, "you will have to find yourself a new ambassador to the UN to make that announcement." That settled it. Funding would not be restarted.

I later asked Nikki why this was a hill she was willing to die on. UNRWA was not really the difference maker, and the issue seemed trivial alongside everything she was accomplishing. Why risk her job on it?

She looked straight at me and said, "I gave a speech to the UN about how UNRWA is a problem, not the solution. I will not go back to that same body and say that it is still a problem but that we will continue to fund it for a little while longer. No one would take the United States seriously again."

Words only matter if you are willing to back them up. Had we decided to restore UNRWA funding even for only a year, it would hardly have elicited a shrug outside the niche pro-Israel community. But in Haley's eyes, the issue was the word of the United States of America. We needed to follow up our speeches with steely resolution—or else we shouldn't bother with the speeches in the first place. Following through isn't necessarily easy, but the principle is certainly not complicated.

Funding of hatred was also targeted in the Anti-Terrorism Clarification Act, signed into law on October 3, 2018. Under this law, entities that accept foreign aid from the United States can be held liable in U.S. courts when U.S. citizens are victims of terror perpetrated by that entity. As a consequence, the Palestinian Authority refuses to accept U.S. aid, which is a stunning admission of guilt. The Anti-Terrorism Clarification Act and the Taylor Force Act were written by Congress to prevent U.S. taxpayer dollars from being used to perpetrate terrorism. These are reasonable laws by any measure. The Palestinian Authority, the entity designated by the West as the peace-pursuing moderates, has not abandoned its practice of martyr payments, and has not reformed its behavior to eliminate the legal risk for inciting and encouraging terrorism. In light of these facts, it is remarkable that there are members of the current U.S. administration and members of Congress who insist that peace can be achieved if the United States funds the PA. They are willing to look the other way and circumvent U.S. law by finding ways to send money to the PA. As long as these voices continue to be part of the mainstream, the PA will not have any incentive to reform.

We have many European allies who are still funding UNRWA and the Palestinian Authority, with full knowledge of what the PA is engaged in. Western democracies appear to have different rules on terrorism. One rule prohibits funding of entities that are engaged in or give support to terrorism. The other rule excuses those who commit terrorist acts against Israel and the Jews. This double standard is anti-Semitism and blatant bigotry. Israel will figure out how to overcome this prejudice and will thrive. But the indulgence of the PA represents a bigotry that is harder to overcome—the bigotry of low expectations that is contained in the assumption that Palestinians are unable to meet the same standard as others.

The Trump peace team, including several Orthodox Jews, knew that Palestinians are bright, capable, and motivated. The team also understood that historical disagreements were not all going to be resolved in a week or even a decade. But it was clear that the trajectory was in the wrong direction, and something needed to change if any progress toward peace and prosperity was to be made. Sweeping PA malfeasance under the rug only reduced the incentive to change leadership and bring a better chance of success to the Palestinian people.

16

NO MORAL EQUIVALENCY

O ne way that Ambassador Friedman demonstrated the principle of standing with our allies was by personally offering
condolences for victims of terror. In the past, some ambassadors
would offer condolences for U.S. citizens killed by terrorism,
though it was not a regular practice. When Friedman arrived
in Israel, he made it a policy that he or I, and often both of us,
would make a condolence call to the family of every single terror victim in Israel. A disproportionate number of these people
lived in the West Bank, where visits involved highly technical
security coordination. Nonetheless, we considered these visits
important, though it wasn't until March 2019 that I fully grasped
the significance.

The ambassador was busy with preparations for a visit by
Mike Pompeo, the secretary of state, when he tasked me with
two condolence visits on the Fast of Esther, the day before Purim.
The first was to the family of a rabbi in the West Bank who had
been gunned down in a terror attack, and the second was to the
family of a twenty-two-year-old soldier killed while trying to
stop that attack. Condolence calls under normal circumstances
are awkward and challenging. Condolence calls in your second

language, when you know that every word will be scrutinized, is one of the most difficult tasks I was called upon to perform.

On the morning of the Fast of Esther, I woke up with a heavy heart. I expected to be in the car for up to seven hours that day and also involved in phone calls about last-minute coordination for Pompeo's visit. I was nervous about how my condolence calls would go, and I didn't have my usual several cups of coffee that morning since I was fasting. I already had a headache and knew it was going to get worse as the day progressed.

Arriving at the first home in an armored four-car motorcade—which I always thought was overkill—I reminded myself that I was representing the United States of America, and that our nation stands with our allies against terror, now and always. I knew that if I sat in the room for ten minutes and said a few comforting words but mostly listened, the visit would go as well as it could.

When I walked in, all other visitors were asked to move to another room, leaving the murdered rabbi's wife, his thirteen children, and their grandparents, all in mourning. The victim's mother-in-law broke down in heaving sobs. I didn't know what to do, but I took the seat reserved for me and said, "Ambassador Friedman apologizes for not being here. He was called away for last-minute preparation for the arrival of our secretary of state. He has sent me here on his behalf and on behalf of President Trump to offer our sincere condolences and to let you know that we stand here with you now and always."

I asked the kids, "Please tell me one thing about your father that I can take with me to preserve his memory." One by one, the thirteen of them thanked me for coming and shared a thought about their father. Since they ranged in age from three to twenty-five, their thoughts and emotions ran the gamut.

Then the mother-in-law told me this was her *second* son-in-law to be murdered by terrorists. She loved her family and her country more than life itself. She mentioned that when she was sitting shiva for her first murdered son-in-law, the international community came out with a statement asking all sides to deescalate the violence. They asked Israel to stop building homes, and Palestinians to stop killing Israelis. Thousands of Israelis came to visit and comfort her and her family, yet she still felt lonely.

When I walked into the room with the American flag pin on my lapel, she couldn't contain her emotions. She then knew that she wasn't alone. She felt that 300 million Americans were standing with her, lending their shoulders for her to cry on. "You have brought me comfort," she said.

I knew what she meant but left unspoken: The most righteous and powerful nation in history was not saying that Jews shouldn't build homes in Judea. Instead, it was saying that terror is inexcusable, and that there is no moral equivalency between the murderers and the murdered.

I am not ashamed to say that I wept along with the mother-in-law. I felt the presence of Pastor Hagee, of my friends from my synagogues across the United States, of ordinary Americans who know the difference between right and wrong. I knew it was the highest honor and greatest privilege to be in that room.

My experience that day is etched in my memory. The time of a government official is precious, and I considered this visit the best possible use of my time as a representative of the United States. It mattered greatly to those who were personally harmed by terror, and the regular policy of condolence calls sent a clear message to the people of Israel and the State of Israel: You are not alone. You will not be alone. The United States will stand by you.

With these visits, we stripped away the moral equivalency that existed in U.S. policy prior to President Trump. We made it clear that we would stand consistently and adamantly against anti-Semitism, not just for the good of the Jewish people but for the good of America. That is what Ambassador Friedman spoke to me about after I said that I was unqualified for the job he was offering because I was an observant Jew. He was determined to confront decades of nefarious moral relativism, and the battle was waged in some unexpected places, from the pages of State Department reports to the homes of terror victims. I'm proud to have been a foot soldier in that battle.

Ending the moral equivalency also worked as deterrence, since it removed constraints on Israel's ability to act in its own defense. The most obvious goal of terrorism is to threaten Israelis physically, but another goal is to garner international sympathy, on the premise that terrorism is a desperate measure taken by the weak. Israelis have proved to be resilient, and terrorist attacks have strengthened their resolve. When the United States is resolute in condemning terror and not the building of homes, the terrorists lose international sympathy. This allows Israel the diplomatic space to take all necessary steps to defend itself—which in turn makes it a valuable ally and force multiplier for the United States.

17

A PURIM TO REMEMBER

The day after my powerful experience in offering condolences was the holiday of Purim. This is the day when Jews around the world celebrate their ancestors' survival of an evil decree by Haman, advisor to the king of Persia in the fourth century BCE, ordering that all Jews be killed. The Jews were saved by the incredible bravery of Queen Esther and her wise mentor Mordechai. Many visitors to the embassy referenced this biblical story, often quoting Chapter 4, verse 14 from the book of Esther: "For if you remain silent at this time, relief and deliverance for the Jews will arise from another place, but you and your father's family will perish. And who knows but that you have come to your royal position for such a time as this?"

Purim in 2019 was also the day that Mike Pompeo arrived in Israel for his second visit as secretary of state and his first to the embassy in Jerusalem. For most of my four years at the embassy I had several conflicting obligations, and as they say, you can only dance at one wedding at a time. I tried to attend as many embassy events as possible. My wife and family understood that this was a unique time in our life and that every morning when I put my American flag pin on my lapel, I was representing the greatest country in the world. They would often run out to greet the driver who was taking me to work that day. Since I was posted to Israel, it was rare that my official responsibilities conflicted with Jewish holidays. It seems that Purim was the one holiday we always had an important visitor coming to town.

During his visit on March 21, Secretary Pompeo would be the first U.S. secretary of state to go to the Western Wall with the prime minister of Israel. By this time I had a pretty firm idea of what my role would be with visitors, and I knew the tradeoff involved in spending time with visiting officials at the expense of other work or time with my family. But if I could be part of planning a historic event, I would do it, and my family would understand. So I had worked with Orit from the Foreign Ministry on the planning for Pompeo's visit.

I started the holy day of Purim dressed as a camel, part of our family's costume theme, which was Arabian Nights that year. We all dressed up in traditional Gulf clothing of some kind, except for Simcha, age eight, who was a ninja. Simcha is always a ninja. I went to the earliest synagogue services to fulfill my religious obligation. Afterward I was picked up at my house, no longer dressed as a camel, to go meet Secretary Pompeo at the embassy. My kids were still in their cute costumes when I kissed them goodbye and wished them a great Purim without me.

I got to the embassy twenty minutes before Pompeo was due to arrive and made sure that everything was just so. As usual, the embassy team had done the preparations perfectly. But when the motorcade pulled up, I didn't recognize most of Pompeo's team or the Israeli security staffing the visit, and I realized that today wasn't going to be my day. I was likely to be outside the security bubble most of the time, which basically meant that I could just as well be running things from my phone anywhere. Ambassador Friedman saw me peering over the security team and pulled me in for a quick hello and a picture with Pompeo beside the embassy's dedication plaque, but then I was bounced to the staff van. It was pleasant enough, though far from an ideal place to accomplish any real work. As the day continued, I remained just outside the bubble. Estee was keeping me abreast of my family's celebrations via WhatsApp, and I began to feel more conflicted about being away from them.

After the official meetings, the Pompeos visited the Church of the Holy Sepulcher, went to the Western Wall with Prime Minister Netanyahu, and finally had dinner with Ambassador Friedman and the Netanyahus. Normally I would have angled to be included, especially since Mrs. Friedman was back in the States, but that night I would be flying there myself to speak at AIPAC, and I wanted to have a little bit of family time before I disappeared for the week. As the motorcade departed for the Church of the Holy Sepulcher, there was a scheduling snafu, so I jumped out of the car to coordinate the rest of the day with the prime minister's team. The shuffle allowed a member of the embassy staff to visit the church as Mrs. Pompeo's staffer. It was my colleague's first time going to the site, and I figured it would make her day. We managed to get the scheduling back on track, and I headed for the Western Wall. I was still outside the bubble, more spectator than participant as the secretary of state made his historic visit to Judaism's holiest site with the prime minister.

Much of what happens on high-level visits is personality-based. The secretary of state travels to dozens of countries and works with thousands of staff around the world. One hotel is like another, one embassy resembles another. I knew that in Israel we were different, but I had thought it would be useful to do some research to find out what I might have in common with Mike Pompeo. After about five phone calls I learned that we had a mutual friend named Adam from Wichita, Kansas. I had done this kind of research before, and sometimes it paid off. Other times when I name-dropped someone, the VIP would pat me on the shoulder, say "Great guy," and move on. By now I wasn't so reliant on this type of "in" as I had been earlier, but I wanted to be prepared if the moment struck.

Prime Minister Netanyahu was jubilant to be at the Western Wall with Friedman and Pompeo, and as a history buff he led them on an informative tour. I had fallen into step with my usual buddies on Netanyahu's team, and we were savoring the moment. At the end of the tour, Netanyahu and Pompeo prayed at the wall, and then there were a few minutes for some photos. Friedman pulled me into the security bubble for a picture at the Western Wall with himself, Netanyahu, and Pompeo. Finally, after a day of running around, I would have something to show that I was part of the event.

You miss 100 percent of the shots you don't take, so as I stood next to Pompeo for the photos, I said to him, "You know who would give his left arm to be in this picture with you and me right now?" The secretary of state is our nation's chief diplomat for a reason. Pompeo didn't roll his eyes, and it was apparent that he correctly assumed there wasn't a long list of people who would want to be in a picture with both of us. "Who would that be?" he asked. "Adam XYZ," I replied. "Yup, great guy," he said, patting me on the shoulder, then turned to the next person in the tiny photo line. I thought to myself, well, clearly Adam is not the friend of Mike that I thought he was, but at least I got my photo and now I'll run home to have the Purim meal with my family before I fly out.

Those thoughts all ran through my head in the split second before Pompeo turned back to me and said, "Wait, you know Adam XYZ?" He grabbed my arm and brought me in for a conversation, and it wasn't superficial. Two fascinating things occurred in those two or three minutes. The first was that while the prime minister was saying goodbye to him, Pompeo basically held me in place. The second was that it became obvious as we walked to the car that Pompeo knew Adam XYZ far better than I did.

I left the Western Wall on a high, feeling that I had indeed spent my time effectively. But the excitement of the day had only begun. Friedman called me to ask if I succeeded in arranging for someone to read the Megilla for him that evening before he departed for the United States. "By the way," he added, "look at the president's tweet." This is what it said: "After 52 years it is time for the United States to fully recognize Israel's Sovereignty over the Golan Heights, which is of critical strategic and security importance to the State of Israel and Regional Stability." My ride back to Raanana became more thrilling than I could have imagined. And for those who are curious, I did succeed in coordinating a Chabad rabbi to read the Megilla for Friedman that evening.

Sovereignty over the Golan Heights was one of the primary issues that the ambassador had wanted to work on after the Jerusalem embassy opening, and it seemed like the easiest. There aren't any Palestinians living there, and the other entity with a claim on the territory is the brutal Syrian regime. Six months earlier it was made clear that Syria didn't even have control of its own side of the border, as ISIS and various other groups fought for control of what had become a no-man's land following the Syrian civil war. Throughout the preceding year, when I brought visitors to the Golan Heights, we could actually see the opposing sides shooting at each other. With that much instability and violence just across the border, there was no way that Israel could relinquish control of such a strategic area. Israel is a small country, and the height advantage of Golan made all the difference in keeping the civil war out of Israel, and probably Jordan. Until rainbows and unicorns reign throughout the land, Israel will never contemplate retreating from the Golan Heights. Even so, recognizing Israeli sovereignty would buck the establishment and it would look like a political gift to Netanyahu, who was facing yet another election.

I had mentioned the issue when I was being trained and briefed at the State Department before I went to the embassy in Tel Aviv. There were senior officials who hoped I would be a counterbalance to what they perceived as a crazy and aggressive ambassador. They were determined to educate me on every terrible scenario that could possibly transpire if the United States recognized Jerusalem as the capital of Israel and moved its embassy there. After about ninety minutes of hearing doom and gloom based on more white papers and position papers than I could count, I said, "Look, I know Ambassador Friedman exceptionally well. He does not want to endanger a single person, and if Jerusalem is truly too dangerous to touch, we should brief him on that, and he will listen. However, the president got elected and appointed David Friedman to execute his policies, and these policies are not going to be the same old same old."

Then I suggested, "How about considering the recognition of sovereignty over the Golan Heights? This is surely less controversial, and by the way, it's not like the Trump administration has given equal weight to both sides of this conflict. President Trump launched fifty-nine Tomahawk missiles at the Syrian regime less than eight weeks ago. I think they are probably 100 percent mad already, and you can't be more than 100 percent mad." The senior briefers promised to think about it and get back to me the next day.

The following day, the State Department trainers in the big conference room seemed to be more interested in seeing how they could work with me. These people had studied the Middle East for years and years. They were the experts. But I knew

David Friedman, and that was the piece of knowledge that no one else in the room possessed. They began by asking if the Golan Heights could really be a substitute for the fulfillment of the Jerusalem Embassy Act. I told them it wouldn't be, unless it was proved that following through with the embassy law would lead to death and destruction. I said that the Golan Heights was a good policy decision if that was the alternative, and I could work on persuading Friedman to save Jerusalem for a second term, or at least when the region settled down more. There was really nothing more entertaining for me than speaking in 2017 about President Trump's second term. It caused visible recoil in people, as though one election was an aberration and there was no chance in the world this disaster could ever happen again. I got the sense from the senior policy folks that if they could just hold on for three and a half years, they could save the world from the duly elected president of the United States.

The senior policy people replied, "Look, Jerusalem is not possible. People will die. And while we value the idea of substituting Jerusalem with the Golan and agree it is less contentious and not likely to cause death and destruction, we cannot support that either. You see, if we take a unilateral position on the Golan Heights, then we will be prejudging the future outcome in negotiations."

I was in shock. We, the United States of America, were concerned about prejudging negotiations between Israel, our closest ally in the Middle East, and the dictator in Syria who is responsible for killing hundreds of thousands of his own people? We wouldn't take a side, or put our thumb on the scale for the future security of the entire Middle East? After a few more minutes of polite conversation, I thanked them all for their time and invited them to come visit at the embassy whenever they wanted. But two things became clearer at that moment. First, they believed there was such a thing as leading from behind. Second, if they were so wrong about the Golan, they were probably wrong about Jerusalem too. I became more convinced than ever that Friedman was the only one seeing things clearly.

By the time Secretary Pompeo visited Israel on Purim in 2019, various people had tried to convince President Trump to recognize Israeli sovereignty over the Golan Heights, but no one had yet succeeded. I don't know if it was the power of prayer at the Western Wall that afternoon on Purim, or the fact that Friedman, Pompeo, Kushner, and others were fully aligned on this issue, or if Friedman once again proved to be the trusted advisor at the exact right time, but the president made yet another decision that further strengthened the U.S.-Israel relationship and brought much-needed clarity to a complicated and confusing region. Someone more politically motivated could have picked a different time or manner for this historic announcement, but that was not the "Friedman way." As I continued to learn from him, when you can do the right thing, always do it, and the timing will take care of itself.

Purim is a holiday where you celebrate the unexpected. God works in wonderous ways, as I was reminded at this moment: Here I am, sitting in a car with the secretary of state and the ambassador to Israel while they are on speaker phone with the president and the recognition of the Golan is being announced on Twitter, and I'm here because I am friends with a guy named Adam from Wichita. Needless to say, my ride back to Raanana to have dinner with my family before a redeye flight took on new meaning as we began to celebrate a Purim miracle, the miracle of real leadership, the miracle of doing the correct thing today because who knows what tomorrow may bring. It was truly a Purim to remember.

18

MISSING THE OPPORTUNITY

W hile the U.S. Embassy was still in Tel Aviv, it had a complicated relationship with the U.S. Consulate in Jerusalem. Normally, embassies are located in a country's capital city, while consulates in other cities serve as branch offices and report to the embassy, which ensures streamlined communication and uniform messaging. But Jerusalem and the consulate were not considered to be under the ambassador's area of responsibility (AOR).

The United States established a consulate in Jerusalem temporarily in 1844 and then permanently in 1857. After the State of Israel was founded in 1948, the United States set up its embassy in Tel Aviv and kept a consulate in Jerusalem, which in U.S. policy was a *corpus separatum*, a separate entity. That remained so after the Six-Day War when Jerusalem was unified under Israeli rule and after Israel applied its sovereignty over all of municipal Jerusalem. Every mission needs a purpose for its existence, and after the Oslo Accords, the U.S. Consulate in Jerusalem became the de facto mission to the Palestinians. The consuls general and their teams in Jerusalem served as the primary interlocutors between the United States and the Palestinian Authority. I am not aware of an occasion when the consulate engaged with the government of Israel, but it did allocate substantial funds to OneVoice, which went on to become V15, a political organization dedicated to the ousting of Netanyahu.

Within the State Department, the U.S. Consulate in Jerusalem was regarded as a crown jewel of diplomatic posts. The people working there could live in a first-world country with every amenity under the sun, including freedom and personal security, and commute by armored car to pursue the noble cause of nation building. It was one of the most sought-after postings in the Middle East. But the consulate made our work at the embassy complicated, if not impossible. The consulate's area of responsibility was Jerusalem, where one finds the Knesset, the Israeli Supreme Court, the president and the prime minister. Whenever embassy staff, including the ambassador, wished to go to Jerusalem, we were supposed to coordinate with the consulate.

The main building of the consulate is on Gershon Agron Street, right across from a fantastic park, 250 meters from the Great Synagogue, very near the prime hotel locations, and less than one kilometer from the official residence of the prime minister. (When President Trump's motorcade left the King David Hotel for the prime minister's residence, the first car arrived before the last one even left the hotel.) It now seems crazy that this facility on Gershon Agron Street served as a mission to the Palestinians. Even if Israel one day finds a true partner for peace on the other side of the negotiating table and chooses to divide Jerusalem—which could happen, though I am highly skeptical—in no circumstances would this location ever be part of any country other than Israel.

Once the embassy was opened in Jerusalem, it made no sense to have a consulate in the same city, with some vague notion of overlapping AORs. Ambassador Friedman now had Mike Pompeo as an ally in Washington, and on March 4, 2019, the consulate in Jerusalem officially merged into the embassy. The old residence of the consul general in Jerusalem became the official residence of the ambassador, fulfilling the final mandate of the Jerusalem Embassy Act: to establish the official residence of the chief of mission to Israel in Jerusalem. With the merger, the United States demonstrated that it does not believe in dividing Jerusalem, unless Israel chooses to do so itself. Finally, staff from the former consulate now worked with embassy staff under one roof and one leader, so it became easier to work together for the benefit of the United States and for all people in the enlarged area of responsibility.

Another result was that Palestinians now had direct access to the U.S. Embassy. For decades, the consulate team patiently heard complaints by Palestinians against the Israeli "occupiers." Some of those complaints had merit and many did not, but all were handled the same way: the consulate officer would write a cable explaining the injustice, which would go back to the main State Department, and eventually the complaint would be translated into talking points for an undersecretary to use in meeting with a counterpart in Israel or at the Israeli Embassy in Washington. Usually there was little movement on these cases because of the roundabout process of communication that resulted from the fact that the consulate in Jerusalem was not accredited to the State of Israel and therefore did not have official contacts with the Israeli government, at least in my experience. Moreover, the consulate did not use the embassy to convey messages effectively because they were not in the same organizational structure. During the Obama years, a fistfight broke out between a U.S. Consulate

Jerusalem officer and a U.S. Embassy Tel Aviv officer about a meeting that was to take place in a suburb of Jerusalem. They were literally throwing fisticuffs over whose AOR the meeting was happening in and who would take the notes and send a cable to Washington.

When the U.S. Consulate merged into the U.S. Embassy, Palestinians could take their complaints directly to the embassy. What's more, David Friedman had better access both to the highest echelons of the Israeli government and to the White House than any ambassador in history. The Palestinians now had a great opportunity, but as Abba Eban famously said, "The Palestinians never miss an opportunity to miss an opportunity."

The Palestinians felt that the merger was such a terrible affront that it was in their interest to boycott the entire U.S. government, which had pumped billions of dollars into their economy and which has more influence over Israel than any other country in the world. This was a miscalculation of leverage. The United States does not need the Palestinians. It cares for them, hopes they will succeed, and will do its best to help them succeed, but it does not need them. The Palestinians do need the United States. By choosing not to speak to the United States in any capacity under the Trump administration, the so-called leaders of the Palestinians only hurt the Palestinian people.

Everyone is entitled to their own narratives, but not their own reality. When the Palestinians were confronted with reality—the reality that the United States is subject to its own laws, such as the Taylor Force Act, the Jerusalem Embassy Act, or the law placing conditions on the Palestinian mission in D.C.—they could have done some reflection, possibly leading to negotiation and compromise. Instead, they refused to engage at all with officials from the Trump administration, insulted the administration, and deflected blame for their own failings. They chose to shrink from the moment. They missed the opportunity. This wrong-headedness continued through the rest of the Trump term. The message from the Palestinians was: if it isn't our way, we aren't going to come to the table. Frankly, the U.S. administration was fine with that. President Trump and his team decided that they were going to work with willing partners, and leave opportunities open for reasonable people to come back to the table if they chose. But they were not going to "pay" to get a party to show up to the table.

19

THE DOOR IS WIDE OPEN

There is an ancient Jewish tradition that God himself comes down into the field to greet his people during the High Holidays. In this auspicious time it is easier than ever to approach him. He has opened the door, and all we need to do is walk through it. The Peace to Prosperity Workshop held in the Kingdom of Bahrain in June 2019 was not just opening the door to the Palestinians. It was paving the road, trimming the grass, sweeping the entry mat, and then keeping the door held open by two valets in morning suits and top hats.

Jared Kushner had partnered with the Kingdom of Bahrain to cohost the conference, held at the magnificent Four Seasons in Manama. Jared and his team brought together regional leadership, sovereign wealth funds, and key international players, ranging from the CEO of AT&T to the chairman of Blackstone. Some of the world's best thinkers and investors came to Bahrain with a concrete plan to invest $50 billion in the region, including not only the Palestinian territories but also Jordan, Lebanon, and Egypt. This would be a comprehensive economic workshop seeking to elevate all people in the region. The atmospherics of this international workshop were important, because the trend lines for President Trump were positive but not unshakable, and the verdict was inconclusive on the untraditional approach to Middle East policy.

The first premise of the conference was that the donor model for Palestinian sustenance was not successful. It bred corruption and kept the Palestinians constantly in need of handouts, robbing a prideful and capable people of self-worth and self-determination. Second, the longstanding approach to negotiations with Palestinians, focusing on confidence-building measures and emphasizing process, was not working. It had stretched on for decades without delivering results. Process without a clear, achievable goal is subject to backsliding and can too easily be hijacked by extremists. Third, it was not possible to resolve all of the political issues of the Israeli-Palestinian conflict at present, but people in the region could still benefit from investments in their communities and businesses. The whole region should not remain paralyzed because some issues cannot be addressed today. Finally, the "blame Israel" strategy of regional players had for too long worked in their interest at home and brought no negative repercussions abroad. Now that strategy would bring a penalty from the United States. On the other hand, acting to improve the lives of the Palestinian people, even without a final political settlement, would have positive ramifications for regional leaders at home and abroad.

The workshop offered a bold proposal, reminiscent of the postwar Marshall Plan, for the region surrounding and including the Israeli-Palestinian areas. Some stellar businesspeople and investors—including John Rader, Thomas Storch, and Scott Leith—laid out a comprehensive investment plan to transform the lives not only of the Palestinian people, but also of Jordanians, Egyptians, Lebanese, and Syrians, if they wish to become part of the solution. One working theory behind the plan was that borders create definition but not necessarily separation, at least in economics. In a geographic region as small as this, the economic plan would elevate all parties that want to be elevated, resulting in a vastly improved regional economy. It was a roadmap for moving a region from being a charity recipient to being an investable economy, and thus empowering its people.

The Peace to Prosperity Workshop involved the top donors to Palestinian causes for the past twenty-five years or more. Many of these countries have also been staunch diplomatic partners of the Palestinians, and some have had bigger internal issues than the Palestinians have. They had grown tired of the perpetual Palestinian problem and knew that there would never be a realistic solution with the existing Palestinian leadership. They were willing to consider another way to be supportive of the Palestinian people.

The conference presented a paradigm shift away from endless charity without results. The United States alone had donated more than $5 billion to the Palestinians since the Oslo Accords, and it was difficult to see evidence that the chance for peace had increased in that time, or to discern a net positive result from the expenditure. In the new paradigm, we would be an investor rather than a donor. When you donate to someone, you may hope they will achieve goals you have agreed upon. When you invest in someone, you have very specific metrics that you need to see, including repayment of your investment. Exponential returns can never be created by charity, but only through intelligent and diligent investment.

In the past, the international donor community was forced to funnel its money through the Palestinian Authority, which would use the funds to solidify its control and secure allegiances. The donations further empowered the Palestinian leadership at the expense of the Palestinian people. The policy of investment rather than donation would require a transparent and fair legal and financial system in the Palestinian territories, and it would enable a broad swath of Palestinians to control their own destiny.

Some thought it wrong for the United States to cut off donations to the Palestinian Authority. Detractors claimed that the decision was biased or even racist. I can attest that President Trump's team did not look down upon the Palestinian people, but regarded them as some of the smartest, most hardworking and entrepreneurial people in the region. The new approach essentially said, "We think highly of you and your potential. Therefore, we want to *invest* in you." This would eliminate the bigotry of low expectations, while offering the Palestinian people more agency and increasing their power to change their own future.

The investment plan unveiled at the conference in Bahrain could boost the entire region. It was both realistic and comprehensive, recognizing that investment was necessary in Jordan and Egypt as well as in the Palestinian territories. It also recognized that some physical and legal infrastructure would need to be in place for the money to be used effectively.

The world's donor community was excited to become an investment community, willing to invest sums of money that wouldn't have been imagined from a donor perspective. Unfortunately, the Palestinian Authority preferred to be an eternal recipient of charity, as did the cottage industry of "human rights" and "peace" groups that lived on the donor model. The PA and Hamas both chose to boycott the workshop. The Palestinian leadership alleged that it was an attempt to "buy them off," but this was only an excuse to boycott it. They claimed that they boycotted the workshop because it focused on economic steps before political steps, which it did. But they really boycotted because a prerequisite to becoming an investment-worthy economy is clear and transparent laws, and little or no corruption. The Palestinian Authority does not have clear and transparent laws, and it is rife with corruption, but the world does not apply pressure to change.

The Palestinian leadership didn't just boycott the conference, but also threatened the few brave Palestinian businessmen who attended the event. They even threatened the host country, Bahrain, as well as the countries that sent representatives. This was a more striking example of chutzpah than Israel has ever displayed. The premise of the conference seems so filled with common sense, yet some thought it so controversial that the road leading to the Four Seasons in Manama was guarded by two armored vehicles of the Bahrain Defense Force.

What's worse, the media fully supported the Palestinian leadership's narrative about the workshop and condemned the hosts, the organizers, and the participants for "selling out" the Palestinians. "Blame Israel" suits the prejudices of media editors around the world and sells well to their audiences, but it does nothing to help the Palestinian people they purport to care about.

My own task for the workshop was to select a small group of Israeli civilians who would be part of the greater Peace to Prosperity project by representing their country well and demonstrating the upside of normalization, and also to find Palestinian civilians who wanted to participate. I recruited eleven Israelis who embody the spirit of the Startup Nation, and they traveled to Bahrain to apply their skills toward elevating their neighbors in the region. This was the first time that Israeli civilians were invited as official guests of the Kingdom of Bahrain. As there was no diplomatic relationship, the visas had to be created specifically for the invitees. These eleven Israelis were adventurous, brave, and excited about the prospect of building a new, better Middle East for all, including their Palestinian neighbors.

One of these people, Netta Korin, called to ask if she should fly on her U.S. or Israeli passport.

I asked her, "What kind of Middle East do you want to see five years from now?"

She replied, "Things won't progress unless I can fly on my Israeli passport." That was that.

I told Netta that everything would be great, and indeed it was.

Bringing Israelis to the conference was not difficult. The challenging part of my job was to bring Palestinians there. Through diligence and diplomacy, Ambassador Friedman cultivated a small but motivated group of Palestinian businessmen who knew that their leadership was the problem. They bravely agreed to attend the conference. The night before they were set to depart for Manama, we had a conference call with them. They asked what kind of protection the United States could provide them. I explained that there were protections we could offer if they chose not to return to the Palestinian territories, but alas there was basically nothing we could do if they went back.

The point of the conference, I stressed, would be to shape leaders who could return home and offer their people a better future and, most importantly, hope. "I don't think anyone should attend the conference without fully understanding the risks involved," I added. "And only you as individuals can properly assess your risk level."

Despite their worries, eight of the eleven invited Palestinian businessmen found the opportunity too alluring to pass up. Upon arriving at the Four Seasons in Manama, they were promptly greeted by the big players with tremendous excitement and respect.

In retrospect, the whole concept seems surreal. The Palestinian businessmen who flew from their cities and villages in the Palestinian territories were not titans of industry, but average people who owned small and mid-sized enterprises. Not to sell them short, but they were not the kind of people you would normally expect to bring about transformational change. Yet for two days they would be rubbing elbows with the heads of the largest wealth funds in the world and political leaders of great stature. Imagine someone who owns two or three small stores being invited to offer tips to Warren Buffett and Jeff Bezos on how to grow a business.

For me, the event was quite moving. It was my first time traveling outside Israel or the United States on official business for the U.S. government. It was also my first visit to a fully Arab or Muslim nation. On the weekend before the workshop I happened to be in the United States getting my family settled at summer camp, so I flew to Bahrain from East Stroudsburg, Pennsylvania. I think I am probably the first person in history to book that particular journey, which took me first from East Stroudsburg to Scranton, then to Dulles in Washington, then to Frankfurt, then on to Riyadh, and finally to Manama.

When I first took my position as senior advisor to Ambassador Friedman, I had expressed to him my concern that wearing a kippa might interfere with my success in the job. He told me that the United States doesn't punish you for your beliefs, and if you are proud of your beliefs they should only help you. Still, my wife had worries about me flying on my own through Saudi Arabia and into Bahrain with a kippa on my head. In fairness to her, a trip like this was not part of my original job description. There is always some anxiety about the unknown, and this was about as unknown as we could have imagined. Estee asked me if I would wear a baseball cap as my head covering in public areas, and I assured her that I would. But we both knew that I was only telling her what she needed to hear, and that I would wear a kippa wherever I went.

I called the U.S. Embassy in Bahrain to ask if wearing a kippa would be an issue. This was the first time they had ever received such a question, I was told, but they thought it should be fine, as Bahrain is well known for tolerance and kindness. This was my first call to the embassy in Bahrain, though I would be working with our team there many times subsequently, and they became some of my favorite colleagues. After assuring Jared that I wouldn't put him in an uncomfortable situation, I took off on the longest flight itinerary I have ever taken, with kosher food in my carry-on, an American flag pin on my lapel, and a kippa on my head. During the brief layover in Riyadh, it was time for morning prayers, so I put on my tallit (prayer shawl) and tefillin (phylacteries) and prayed. Aside from a few glances, perhaps a stare or two, everything went fine.

In Bahrain, the Israelis were welcomed royally as a guest of the king himself. The conference included some of the kindest and most engaging leaders from the region I had ever met. While the security was conspicuous at the Four Seasons in Manama, the atmosphere at the workshop was supercharged and purpose-driven. One day I walked into the main lobby and saw two senior players from the American powerhouse Blackstone—including my good friend Eli Miller, who had previously been Secretary Mnuchin's chief of staff—talking with two Palestinian business-men, an Israeli venture capitalist, and the largest Emirati real estate developer. I walked over with my kippa on my head and got the biggest hugs from the Emirati developer and the Pales-tinian shoe manufacturer. It was entertaining to watch Eli do a doubletake at the sight.

The workshop had many highlights, but one that stands out was when the Kingdom of Bahrain asked Jason Greenblatt and me if we would bring any Jewish participants who were interested to their synagogue for morning prayer. It would be the first public prayer service at the synagogue in decades, and the Bahrainis were honored and excited to be able to host us there. It was a joyous and meaningful prayer experience, and also poetic. In many of our prayers we ask for peace, shalom. I say the words many times in a day without really thinking about peace. I have my own everyday problems, like anyone else, and I pray with those in mind. But here in Bahrain, in a synagogue that hadn't been used for a very long time and was opened because the king wanted his Jewish guests to feel welcome, I prayed consciously for peace, perhaps for the first time, and I have been doing so ever since.

The Kingdom of Bahrain showed courage in hosting the workshop. Even more courageous were the Palestinians who attended. There was a feeling all around that the region had the ability to turn a page in its history. A way forward was prepared, and it was now only a question of when the people of the region would come together and move toward a more prosperous and peaceful future. But my conversation with the Palestinian businessmen at the end of the convention threw some cold water on my enthusiasm.

Jason Greenblatt and I met with those eight Palestinians in a conference room on the twenty-first floor of the Four Seasons to talk about the future of the Middle East and discuss the pros and cons of the conference. We asked what the key takeaways were from the Palestinian perspective. The conversation was stilted and awkward, and not because of the language gap, since everyone had been communicating with some form of translation service. There was something else that just wouldn't come out. We were going in circles.

After an hour of this awkward chitchat, at about 10:30 p.m., I realized that I would miss my Pegasus Airlines flight back to Israel via Turkey if I didn't leave soon. I thanked the Palestinians for their courage, their vision, and their commitment to a better and brighter future. I also pledged to meet with them in Jerusalem before long.

As I stood up, the Palestinians did too, but instead of shaking hands and wishing me well in return, they looked Jason and me in the eye and asked us to save them and their families. I will never forget the look of grown men, most of them at least fifteen years my senior, pleading for help. While they were in Bahrain, the message had been delivered to them that their participation wasn't merely frowned upon, it was considered treacherous, and that they and their families would pay for it. With tremendous pain, I reiterated what I had told these brave people before they embarked on their trip to Bahrain: They were taking a risk and we were limited in what we would be able to do when they returned to their homes in the Palestinian territories. These grown men were resolute in their decisions, but understandably terrified. The shame of this is that their supposed crime was attending a conference to learn how they might contribute to improving their cities and communities, and perhaps someday their own state.

The more progress was made for the region, the harder the PA leadership seemed to dig in their heels. Some of the world's top investors came to Bahrain prepared to offer $50 billion of investment in the region, but the primary beneficiaries did not show up because they were insulted. They even resorted to threatening methods I had hoped would not be part of anyone's leadership strategy at this time in history. The workshop was broadcast around the world. The plan is still available online. The Palestinian people know there is an opportunity for them, a better way for their future, but their leaders either don't care or don't want that future. The door is wide open. They just need to walk through it.

I needed to be in Israel the day after the Bahrain workshop to host Nikki Haley and attend a big event at the City of David. Getting from Bahrain to Israel was not easy. Three Israelis had flown to Bahrain on private jets, and they offered rides back to those who had arrived on commercial flights. They would make a thirty-minute stop in Jordan, but would not have to deplane. I was generously offered a ride too, as my commercial flight had me leaving the conference earlier than would be prudent, and would involve a lengthy stopover, making for an eighteen-hour trip whereas a private flight would take two and a half hours.

Here's the catch: I was not permitted to receive a gift of a private flight. So I called the State Department ethics officer and asked if I could pay for the equivalent of first-class fare to the plane owner, and then I would get to work on time the next day. Unique circumstances sometimes call for a little bit of flexibility. "We think we can do it," came the reply. "Hang on." I took their response as a yes, so I didn't go to the airport to catch my original commercial flight through Jordan. Then I was informed that I could go on a private plane if I paid the entire cost of the flight, but even then I would need to get permission in writing a week in advance. Well, that wasn't helpful, so I turned to my colleagues in the Manama embassy, and they helped me get a 2 a.m. flight on a discount airline with a stopover in Turkey. It would take ten hours instead of eighteen, so I was ready to try it.

The Manama embassy team took me to the airport, and the security team provided by the embassy walked me to the gate. It was after midnight, and having gone through the security check, I was in what's considered the safest part of an airport, so I told the security people they could go home. I had about ninety minutes until boarding, and I decided to wander the secure area for that time. It took about ninety seconds for me to realize that there were only two other flights taking off at that hour, one to Afghanistan and the other to Pakistan. And I was wearing a kippa. While Bahrain had been wonderfully hospitable, I was aware that perhaps not everyone who flies in and out of the country was so enlightened. Remembering my promise to Estee, I started looking for a baseball cap. Unfortunately, the one I had brought along was my U.S. Embassy Jerusalem cap, but it did result in an interesting encounter. A twenty-year-old from Oman who was about to board a flight to Afghanistan wanted a selfie with me. He said that he loved the United States and was going to Afghanistan to fight. I didn't ask whom he was going to fight for or against, but simply wished him a safe trip and then walked briskly back to my gate.

When boarding time came, I was curious to see what a discount regional carrier looks like in this part of the world. I found my seat and saw chewing gum all over the cushions. Disgusted, I reached into my pocket for some tissues and gingerly started to pick at the gum. The more I pulled off, the clearer it became that the gum was not there by accident. It was actually holding the seat cushion together. Ten hours later I arrived at Ben Gurion Airport, went straight to the nearest restroom, changed into the extra clothes I had in my carry-on, and dumped everything I had worn on the plane into the nearest garbage can. I must have looked extremely suspicious going into an airport restroom wearing one set of clothes and coming out in another, but I did what had to be done!

20

PILGRIMAGE ROAD

———

Archeologists worked for six long years to excavate the ancient road that led from the Pool of Siloam to the site of the Temple of King Solomon (currently the Western Wall Plaza). One team was digging from north to south, and another from south to north. On June 30, 2019, there was a big celebration to mark the completion of the Pilgrimage Road excavation. Mrs. Netanyahu attended the breakthrough ceremony, along with the former mayor of Jerusalem, Nir Barkat (then a member of the Knesset), and many of the biggest donors to the City of David project. Ambassador Friedman led a U.S. delegation including other ambassadors that we had become friendly with over the prior two years, members of Congress, and White House officials.

It was a scorching day, and as we waited by the Pool of Siloam for the ceremony to begin, I realized that this was going to be a two-suit event at minimum for me. Few people wear suits and ties in Israel, even among elected leaders, but I regularly wore a suit, a tie, and a lapel pin as my uniform to represent the United States. Nearly every day for four years, I was likely to be one of only two people wearing a suit in the whole country of Israel, the other one being the prime minister. On this particular day in June, I knew that I would need to change clothes before the celebratory dinner that evening, because my light gray suit was going to be a very dark gray by the end of the ninety-minute outdoor ceremony.

With much fanfare, Ambassador Friedman and the U.S. delegation then went underground and walked hand in hand on the Pilgrimage Road with the Israeli dignitaries as well as leaders and supporters of the City of David project. At the midpoint, they broke through the temporary wall separating the northern and southern parts of the excavation. Then the small crowd of about a hundred continued on as far as the excavation had been completed. Aside from the archeologists, we were the first people to walk the whole 500 meters of the Pilgrimage Road, on the ancient stones of the very same road that our physical or spiritual ancestors walked on to reach the Temple. It felt as though we had been transported back in time, and every stone our feet touched had a story to tell. This stone is where the prophet told his prophecy, and this one is where children would sit and play while their parents purchased the necessities for Temple services. In these moments we all celebrated the shared values of our two great countries, the United States and Israel.

The celebration concluded with a dinner at the Jerusalem home of David and Tammy Friedman. Benjamin and Sarah Netanyahu were there, along with the U.S. delegation. The fact that the ambassador's home was now on Gershon Agron Street in Jerusalem made it all the more meaningful. I was chosen to be the master of ceremonies, and I can still remember the flutter in my stomach as I got up to address the crowd for the first of many times that evening. There is a certain protocol involved when you have high officials present, and I realized that I hadn't run my planned remarks by any of the protocol team or even the ambassador. I took a deep breath and walked to the stage. Looking out at the audience from the podium, I remembered why I didn't need to clear my remarks. We had done something that was so fundamentally correct that everyone in the room felt the righteousness of their participation. Title and rank took second place to shared values and the project of uncovering history, so I could address the assembled dignitaries as friends.

While I said a lot of words that evening, there is one message that stands out in my memory. In introducing the prime minister, I shared these words of the Prophet Zechariah: "Old men and old women will again sit along the streets of Jerusalem, each with a staff in hand because of great age. And the streets of the city will be filled with boys and girls playing there." Then I described two pictures that hang over my fireplace.

One picture shows my family at the Western Wall, including my parents, along with Benjamin Netanyahu and David Friedman. This photo was taken by Matty Stern, the longtime embassy photographer, on the fourth night of Chanukah in 2018. It was the very first time that any Israeli prime minister had been to the Western Wall with any foreign diplomat. In that picture I see my mentors and heroes epitomizing leadership on the streets of Jerusalem, in an echo of the "old men and women" from Zechariah. The other picture was taken on my family's twelfth visit to the City of David and the Pilgrimage Road (not yet fully excavated). I was probably on a tour with some important U.S. dignitary, and my kids always jumped at the chance to come along with me to the site. Even so, when you're under twelve years old and on your twelfth visit, perhaps you don't want to hear the same narrative yet again, but play around in the excavation instead. Gila, who is always with our family when we go to the City of David, made sure the kids wouldn't break any ancient artifacts as she led them in spirited games of tag, hide-and-seek, and an elaborate form of patty-cake. While they were all seated on the road playing their clapping game, I captured this unique moment of pure joy on their faces. This photo brings to life the words of Zechariah: "And the streets of the city will be filled with boys and girls playing there." Very likely, the prophet had in mind the road that my kids were sitting on. They could very well have been the first to play on it since the destruction of the Second Temple in Jerusalem nearly two thousand years ago.

After explaining these two pictures to the dinner guests, I thanked the prime minister for helping to bring part of Zechariah's prophecy to life. Then I thanked Ambassador Friedman and President Trump for enabling the second half of the prophecy to come to fruition.

I remember sitting at a table in the ambassador's garden with Victoria and George Coates, Ambassador George and Mary Glass, Jason Greenblatt, and Senator Lindsey Graham. The senator was in fine form, regaling the table with story after story. The wine was flowing and everyone was in great spirits. Then almost everyone started getting a flurry of Twitter notifications. The elite media were weighing in on the opening of the Pilgrimage Road, none too pleased with the substantial American presence. In fact, journalists accused Ambassador Friedman and the delegation of essentially taking a sledgehammer to homes in Silwan, just above the excavation.

I am not claiming that the excavation has gone perfectly, without causing structural issues for any homes, but I am quite sure that those running the City of David project made great efforts to accommodate the needs of every resident in the area, whether Jewish, Christian, or Muslim. And while journalists were quick to describe the homes there as Palestinian, Silwan is firmly in Jerusalem; Israel recognized all of Jerusalem as part of Israel; and the United States now recognized Jerusalem as the capital of Israel. But the media, being in love with its own narratives, claimed that the U.S. delegation was literally supporting the destruction of Palestinian homes.

Those news stories bounced rapidly around the Twittersphere, and the echo chamber amplified the message. Yet no one at the celebration that evening seemed to be bothered by it. Everyone there knew they had participated in something positive and truthful.

A fascinating coda to this story took place two months later, during a New Year's toast at the ambassador's home in Herzliya. At such events I tired to meet as many people as possible and present myself as a conduit to the ambassador and the embassy leadership. One of the people I met was an accomplished and articulate lady with kids the same age as mine, and we quickly bonded over the exhilarating experience of living as Americans in Israel, where nearly every day can be a new adventure if you choose. I asked her what her family's favorite place in Israel had been, and she promptly replied, "The Pilgrimage Road at the City of David is the single greatest place my kids and I have been in Israel. It is truly incredible." I could hardly keep from laughing, since her husband was the ringleader of the most disingenuous journalists covering the Pilgrimage Road breakthrough. Even though I had clearly heard her statement, I asked her to repeat it. I was pleased that we indeed had much in common. The next time I saw her husband, I asked him, "Is it awkward when you go to sleep at night?" He knew exactly what I meant, and his answer was refreshingly direct: "I have to write what my readers want to read."

My point isn't to dump on that journalist specifically, or journalism in general, but to illustrate how ingrained narratives are nearly impossible to overturn, even when truth looks you straight in the eye. Going against the conventional wisdom takes courage and conviction, and it takes commitment to truth. You will take arrows for it, but when truth is on your side, history will prove you correct.

In 2020, Ambassador Friedman and Paul Packer, the chairman of the Commission to Preserve Heritage Abroad, recognized the City of David and the Pilgrimage Road as a heritage site with special significance to the United States. This took an enormous amount of effort for one of many archeological sites in Israel. The City of David is not only the historical and spiritual foundation of the modern State of Israel, but also foundational to America's ideals and values. That's why it was so important for the administration to be clear about the cultural value of the City of David and the Pilgrimage Road.

Another story illustrating the importance of the site occurred when I brought Steven Mnuchin there. He is a brilliant person, with a keen eye toward history and the importance of the United States leading the way. As Zeev Orenstein led the tour, Mnuchin peppered him with questions that made the visit come to life even more than usual. One part of the narration tells about the destruction of Jerusalem by the Romans in 70 CE and about coins that archeologists found in the sewers under the Pilgrimage Road. The coins bear the inscription *Judea Capta*, "the Jews have been captured," and depict a Roman soldier standing with his sword upraised over a cowering woman and a child. Zeev said to Steven, "Mr. Secretary, you tell me who won the war." I have been on this tour with Zeev at least twenty-five times, and he always asks that question at that same point. The answers are always interesting, but Steven's was especially so: "The good guys ultimately prevailed," he answered. "How do we know that?" Zeev asked. Without skipping a beat, Steven said emphatically, "Because it is my name on the U.S. currency, and the United States is the most powerful country in the history of the world, and we stand today and will always stand with Israel, and I sign the money." The Jewish people had returned to their ancestral land of Israel and rebuilt their capital on the exact same spot as ancient Jerusalem, and now the United States of America, the world's superpower, embraced and supported Israel in Jerusalem. While the American system of governance owes much to the ancient Romans, the United States must never be Israel's oppressor, but always an ally that honors a shared historical legacy.

Mnuchin's words conveyed the truth that we are part of a larger story. We all have a mission, and we must play our roles to their maximum. I have often felt that the United States and Israel are both not replicable, and that both have a sense of almost prophetic destiny attached to them. Mnuchin's remarks reflected a similar thought, and also spoke instinctively to the *kishka* test: Will the United States stand with Israel? I am not arguing that the United States should support another country when it is not in our best interest. I am making the case that instinctively knowing the correct action to take is a necessary trait in good leadership.

21

WHO WILL OWN
THE FUTURE?

The U.S.-Israel relationship has always had a foundation of shared values, as well as security and intelligence sharing. In the past few years, a new component has become crucial, and it concerns the question of who will dominate the technologies of the future. Strengthening the U.S.-Israel relationship in the context of that global competition will pay dividends for decades to come. President Trump understood, and articulated, better than those who came before him that the United States was not on cruise control to permanent world leadership. Indeed, the United States has many adversaries around the world, including North Korea, Russia, Venezuela, and radical Islamic groups, but none of these were thought to present the same level of threat that the Chinese Communist Party does today. Countless decisions by the Trump administration revolved around this threat, changing the roles of our embassy teams around the world, as every one of our relationships played a part in the competition for supremacy.

In this competition, the United States has the moral high

ground. What's more, a free society should yield the most creativity and ingenuity in developing new technologies. But China has three distinct advantages. 1) The sheer size of the country: The Chinese can dedicate resources toward technological progress at a larger scale than all other countries combined. 2) Intellectual dishonesty: While the United States and most other Western countries abide by many different laws protecting innovation, patents, trademarks, and so on, China doesn't even have such laws, nor does the Chinese Communist Party respect the laws of other countries, including the United States, in their international commercial agreements. 3) Long-term planning: The CCP envisions the future in 100-year plans. Most U.S. administrations have two-year plans taking them to the next midterm election. In the best-case scenario, those plans can be extended into an eight-year plan, though this has rarely been the case, as priorities shift in response to political imperatives. China's leaders are not troubled by day-to-day politics and therefore keep their eye on the 100-year prize, which includes dominance in technologies of the future.

Technologies such as 5G, quantum computing, metadata, hyperspeed, and more will be key to global leadership in the way that gunpowder, assembly lines, automobiles, and airplanes were in the past. They represent the next major world revolution in technology, and getting ahead of it will determine superpower status for the next century. For the United States to continue leading the world, it needs to harness every resource it can in the technology competition, including its alliances.

In the great competition between the United States and China, it is increasingly important for countries and companies to choose sides. This imperative came into sharp perspective with China's quest to "own" the 5G network implementation globally through Huawei and ZTE. It is assumed that these companies, both aligned with the Chinese government, were offering highly subsidized prices for the 5G rollout process in other countries so the CCP could own all of the data that runs through those countries in perpetuity. Those big subsidies were actually a low price to pay for dominance in the world of data. The Trump administration sent out cables to all U.S. embassies worldwide telling them to communicate to their host countries that committing to a Chinese-owned 5G network would necessitate that the United States rethink our intelligence sharing with that country.

This is where the rubber meets the road for a country such as Israel, whose prime minister has proudly and repeatedly declared it the greatest friend that the United States has. If other countries hear that assertion, they may look to Israel to determine how they should navigate the great power competition between the United States and China. If they see Israel choosing America's side, they may be encouraged to follow suit. But if Israel does otherwise, they might think, "If Israel can engage in x y or z with China and still remain the best friend of the United States, then certainly we can engage in x y or z with China as well." That choice can have harmful consequences for small countries in the long term, however. U.S. embassies around the world began having these conversations in earnest in 2018.

Because of Ambassador Friedman's special relationship with the president specifically and the White House in general, leaders from several countries engaged with me on various issues, some but not all related to Israel. I explained as best as possible the United States' concerns about the practices of many Chinese firms doing business overseas. I was not sure if my message resonated, as the embassy had no mechanism for following up on issues not related to Israel. But I was gratified by what I heard in May 2020 when I made phone calls about repatriating Israelis from some of those countries. Some of the same leaders I had spoken with earlier thanked me for protecting their country from the negative effects of doing deals with China.

Ambassador Friedman and I spent a lot of time speaking to Israelis about the challenges and risks involved in dealing with Chinese companies or accepting Chinese investments. We had disagreements, some loud and vigorous, but always behind closed doors. Best friends can argue respectfully and confidentially, while also looking out for each other. Friedman set the policy of never negotiating through the media. When we needed to speak with our allies, we did so directly and clearly. We won most debates, we lost some, but the relationship continued to strengthen. This was in no small part due to the discretion kept by the senior principals in the room, who saw their mission as almost sacred and would not risk it for a moment of fame.

In various technologies of the future, breakthroughs will come from China and Russia, or from the United States and Israel. China will overpay to invest in technology; it will not open its market in a fair way. What's more, China's immigration policy currently gives it a big advantage in attracting talent from Israel, because it is far easier for Israelis to get a visa to China than to the United States. This is especially true for recent graduates of the Israel Defense Forces. The default position of the U.S. consular service is that people who enter the United States will choose to remain unless there is a strong indication that they would feel compelled to return to their home country. This is a reasonable assumption regarding people from most other countries. Many young Israelis like to travel for six months after completing their mandatory service in the IDF, to decompress and regain some of their youth before going on to university or a vocation. The U.S. consular service views most of the people in this group as not having strong enough ties to Israel that they will likely return there rather than stay in the United States. Consequently, they are subject to a higher-than-average rejection rate for visas. The Chinese government default is that recent graduates of the IDF are likely to be startup entrepreneurs in the next few years, so every single applicant from this group receives a visa.

One of the most positive news items I have read from the Biden administration is its move toward adding Israel to the visa waiver program, making it easier for Israelis to travel to the United States. Especially in light of the crisis at our southern border, it's absurd that citizens of our top ally in the Middle East and a major economic driver for our country face a waiting list of more than a year for a U.S. visa appointment. In the global competition for talent, we should make coming to the United States easier for those likely to contribute much to our economy and society.

The United States has an open and fair free market economy and therefore will not be able to compete with China in some ways, so it needs to move closer to Israel and narrow the space for China to outcompete. Israel has rapidly become a world leader in innovation and technology. By standing close with Israel in all capacities—intelligence, defense, diplomacy—the United States places Israel's emerging technologies firmly on the side of good. In my conversations with minister-level leaders from around the world during the pandemic, I heard more than once that the world's hope for rapid innovation in fighting Covid-19 was likely to come from the United States or Israel. If these two countries work closely together to achieve breakthroughs in other areas too, the sky is the limit. If they do not, they are destined to see what life is like when other countries are the superpowers.

This is one reason why it is fully in the interest of the United States to stand resolutely with Israel. When we think of our relationship with an ally like Israel, we naturally assume that the drivers will be our foreign policy teams, our intelligence agencies, and our Defense Department. This is only part of the picture, though. The United States and Israel have touchpoints in many other arenas. Our departments of Energy, Treasury, Homeland Security, Commerce, Transportation, the EPA, and other agencies were involved on a daily basis with their counterparts in Israel strengthening the relationship, and in so doing, strengthening the United States. One basis of the relationship is common values, but another is shared priorities, above all ensuring that we are both victors in the global competition for technological power. More and more parts of the U.S. government looked to Israel as a key asset in this competition. Leader after leader made the trip to Israel, working with our embassy to maximize the benefit of the relationship. If not for the Covid travel restrictions in 2020, far more high-level visitors from across the administration would have come as well.

22

REVISITING
RESOLUTION 242

B y the fall of 2019, the U.S. economy had reached levels not seen before in my lifetime. Everyone who wanted a job could get one, and wages were growing for the lower and middle classes faster than for the wealthy. The economy was on track for record success, and the fundamentals were there for it to be long-term. The United States was not engaged in any significant ground wars abroad, Afghanistan and Iraq seemed to be mostly stabilized, the ISIS caliphate was destroyed, and while there were crises in Venezuela and Lebanon, neither seemed to be headed toward where U.S. troops would be necessary or wanted. If you believe in trendlines, the Trump administration was trending positively. You wouldn't believe that from any of the headlines, or the impeachment hearing that was about to occur, but the average American who was not glued to partisan news or Twitter was pretty pleased with how things were going.

In the Middle East and related policy, President Trump had recognized Jerusalem as the capital of Israel, moved the U.S. Embassy to Jerusalem, merged the U.S. Consulate Jerusalem with the embassy, recognized Israeli sovereignty over the Golan Heights, signed the Taylor Force Act, cut off funding for UNRWA, supported Israel at the UN, left the disastrous Iran deal and imposed crippling sanctions on the terror-supporting Iranian regime, and cohosted the Peace to Prosperity Workshop in Bahrain.

Pundits kept asking what Israel would be giving up in return, but that was the wrong question. The right question was what the United States had given up by not taking those actions before. Every one of them went against the grain of the expert class, but fully comported with reality. The Golan Heights is a strategic location in a tumultuous neighborhood. If Israel were not there permanently, the result would be deadly not just for Israel but for Jordan and eventually for us. History has proved time and again that terrorist groups with enough room will grow and eventually come and attack us. Israel is very good at keeping terrorist entities busy figuring out how to survive, but as soon as this was no longer a concern for them, their ability to wreak havoc elsewhere would be greatly elevated.

Jerusalem was, is, and likely always will be the capital of Israel. Refusing to acknowledge it is akin to my daughter closing her eyes and pretending that whatever scares her is not there, except that it has broader consequences. When the United States faces reality and acts with conviction, the rest of the world takes note. Some countries will follow, and at the every least, the paradigm will have been changed.

All of those actions were undeniably fantastic for Israel, but because they came from Trump, an America First president, it was clear to Americans and others that these were not political moves or gifts, but the correct decisions for the United States of America. President Trump ran on an American First agenda, and foreign policy decisions were viewed through that prism.

The policies themselves are popular in Congress and among the American people. The question isn't so much why President Trump made these decisions as why previous presidents did not, and in some cases did not fulfill their promises. President Trump was not swayed by any of the arguments against making these policy decisions. His view was that if the policies were in the best interest of the United States, then the decision was simple.

By the late 2019, President Trump was already the greatest friend Israel had ever had in the White House, by a wide margin. In addition, the trendlines in the whole region were headed toward a breakthrough, but there were still two obstacles to be surmounted before the president's Deal of the Century could be unveiled. First, Israel needed a stable government; it had been continuously in elections or the threat of elections since early 2018. Frustratingly, it seemed as though the government had consensus on policy, yet conflicts of politics and personality made it unstable. Second, it was necessary to revise some premises if Israel could be confident in coming to negotiations. As Ambassador Friedman was fond of saying, you cannot ask a thief to come to the table to negotiate the terms of his own guilt, but that is basically what was being asked of Israel.

From the Oslo Accords until the Trump administration, the consensus of the international community as well as U.S. negotiators had been that the West Bank was illegally occupied Palestinian territory—that the Israelis had unlawfully conquered it in the Six-Day War of 1967 and needed to return most if not all of it in accordance with UN Resolution 242. This is an extreme interpretation of the resolution, which in a basic reading calls for the return of "territories occupied in the recent conflict." Every word of that resolution was negotiated, and since it doesn't say "all" territories, a reasonable interpretation is that Israel is not required to return all of the territories, but only some. By 2019,

Israel had returned more than 85 percent of the territory it had conquered in 1967, including the Sinai Peninsula and the Gaza Strip. Nearly everyone accepted the premise that Israel would have to give back at least 95 percent of the West Bank, with perhaps a few mutually accepted land swaps, yet this was not at all realistic. Before Israel left Gaza in 2005, it was possible, if naïve, to think that a full surrender of territory could lead to peaceful relations between neighbors. After more than a decade of witnessing the Gaza experiment gone horrifically wrong, it is criminally stupid to believe you would get a better result in the West Bank.

Ambassador Friedman summed it up artfully "If Israelis are to be secure in coming to the table, they cannot be cast as thieves negotiating their own sentence." With this in mind, Ambassador Friedman and Secretary Pompeo had the State Department reevaluate its legal outlook on Israeli civilian settlements in the West Bank. They both dedicated a huge amount of time and energy to making sure they received full buy-in from the State Department legal team, which then produced a legal memo that brought back room for other reasonable interpretations of UN Resolution 242. It addressed the current reality, and stated that the settlements are not per se illegal. This was neither a slam-dunk for the right wing nor a defeat for the left. It did create the opportunity for Israel to come to a negotiating table confident of an outcome that would respect the spirit and language of Resolution 242, and not the pernicious narrative that had prevailed since the Oslo Accords.

Mike Pompeo announced the new position on the settlements at a press conference from the State Department on November 18, 2019. Over in Israel, where it was 6 p.m., I was sitting in the Seaside Conference Room of the embassy branch office in Tel Aviv with David Friedman and David Milstein, his special assistant, who is incredibly fluent in many of the nuances of policy surrounding the U.S.-Israel relationship. We were bracing for fierce pushback to what became known as the Pompeo doctrine. We listened to the announcement and waited for the press inquiries to come in. There were only three. Then David and I went to the soccer match of the year in Israel, Argentina versus Uruguay, which was Messi's first match in Israel.

David Friedman, Morgan Ortagus and I spoke with many of the serious reporters who cover this region, explaining the reasoning behind the memo and answering their questions. These people were briefed in advance because Friedman and Pompeo understood that this was a niche issue and that most of the world would be taking cues from the subject matter experts. Consequently, the reaction was surprisingly muted aside from a flurry of criticism by the usual suspects on Twitter. There are two important reasons for this. First, the Pompeo doctrine made sense. It acknowledged reality and did not pull the issue to an extreme, but brought it back to where it always should have been—in the middle, and in dispute. Second, the announcement came from the secretary of state at the podium in the State Department, quoting a memo that the legal department had developed. This was not Friedman in Israel making up policy, nor Trump tweeting something, but the official center of U.S. foreign policy presenting what appeared to be a carefully calculated policy opinion. The world collectively shrugged. This was remarkable, given that eighteen months earlier the press and social media had made an enormous amount of noise over the embassy's changes to some of the basic language in the State Department reports on human rights and religious freedom. Now the State Department came out with a legal memo that fundamentally changed the narrative of Israel and the West Bank (Judea and Samaria), and the response was mostly silence.

At the same time, people following the matter closely, especially in Israel, felt acknowledged in a meaningful way. There are over 450,000 Jews living in Judea and Samaria. Most of them are not going anywhere. Most of their settlements—or rather, their villages, towns, and cities—are likely to grow and develop further. Many of the Israeli-owned businesses in those areas provide good employment opportunities for Palestinians in close proximity to their homes. Just as the Gaza disengagement brought harm to Palestinians in Gaza, wholesale disengagement from the West Bank would likewise hurt the Palestinian people. The absurdity of calling Jews living in the area, their homes and their businesses illegal from the perspective of the United States is over. Working together, Pompeo and Friedman brought clarity to an issue that had caused confusion for over fifty years.

23

PEACE TO PROSPERITY

"**P**eace to Prosperity: A Vision to Improve the Lives of the Palestinian and Israeli People" was released to the public on January 28, 2020. Before then, senior members of the administration had spoken publicly about Israel and the Palestinians and had sketched rough outlines of what a path forward might possibly look like, but no specifics about the Vision ever leaked. The document existed only on an airlocked computer that was never placed in a vulnerable position. The reason for the secrecy was not that it contained anything that would really shock anyone, but rather because it was complicated. It was not a one-pager with big platitudes that everyone could agree on at first and then fight over later on. It was comprehensive and covered topics that had traditionally been considered final status questions, to be addressed only after every other box had been checked. The peace team took the opposite approach, tackling the thorny issues thoughtfully and in detail, to facilitate progress in all the other areas.

At the beginning of this process, the American team for what Trump called the Deal of the Century consisted of Jason Greenblatt, Jared Kushner, David Friedman, and Avi Berkowitz.

Up to the rollout, there were never more than fifteen people involved. The team that focused on the Vision, and later the Abraham Accords, was unusually small for this file. When I was originally hired for my embassy job, it was to focus on all of the other bilateral issues between Israel and the United States, freeing up the ambassador's time for the highest level of issues. I was a likely addition to the peace team—I think I was the seventh member—but I got there in an unlikely way.

The Peace to Prosperity team tried to have all discussions face to face, and the actual writing of the Vision would be done only on the one airgap computer. For over twenty months I served as a trusted courier flying to and from the States without knowing what was in the sealed envelopes or the locked computer I was carrying. In the earlier part of 2019, it became harder for Friedman to travel on short trips, so I was read into the file almost by default and then wound up flying to Washington for meetings and language insertion. Sometimes I spent 25 hours in transit for 75 minutes of meetings, but we treated this as a once-in-a-lifetime opportunity, and we knew that timing and discretion were crucial for even the smallest chance of success.

There was no perfect time for a rollout. A good time was certainly possible, but it was becoming more difficult to find. By January 2020, the peace team had a decision to make: It was either now, or in the second term if Trump won. Israel was still politically unstable, and the peace team was going to need full buy-in from both Netanyahu and General Benny Gantz, who were political competitors. It was a challenging time to work with both of them on the opportunity that the Peace to Prosperity Vision provided for the region as a whole and for Israel specifically. It could easily turn into a political football, which would not only doom any possible deal, but probably ruin the concepts at its heart.

Jared and David decided they could handle the Israeli politics, or if not, they could live with the possible negative fallout, because nearly everything else that mattered had come into shape. President Trump, even while undergoing an impeachment process, was riding as high as he would throughout his presidency. His foreign policy, while not winning many accolades, was being acknowledged and digested. Arguably his leverage and influence were at an all-time high.

Jared Kushner, arguably the most influential person in America, had spent an enormous amount of time and personal capital on building and developing relationships in the Gulf. To people who follow the Middle East through the lens of Israel or the Israeli-Palestinian conflict, it was not well known that the U.S. relationships with the countries of the Gulf Cooperation Council (GCC) were in need of repair following the Obama administration. Jared, assisted first by Jason Greenblatt and later by Avi Berkowitz, developed respectful relationships with the leadership of many countries in the Middle East and North Africa, the MENA region. They cultivated trust by spending a lot of time listening to MENA leaders' views on the status of the region. They took care to balance the particular needs and interests of the various individual countries, all with long and complicated histories and interrelationships.

While the poll numbers didn't indicate overwhelming approval, the state of play in the United States between foreign policy and the greatest economy in my lifetime gave us the feeling that Trump was rolling toward a second term, barring a black swan event. Add in the actions taken for the U.S.-Israel relationship and Kushner's equity built up throughout the Middle East, North Africa, and beyond, and the only reason not to release the Peace to Prosperity Vision in January was Israeli political instability, and that seemed like a terrible reason to put it back in the drawer, possibly forever. The president gave the green light, and the team led by Jared and David went into full speed. Rollouts of big initiatives may take months of preparation, but this one happened, as I recall, only eight days after the decision to move forward. Getting everything ready took fancy footwork. Avi engineered the final product of the Vision and was responsible for the media rollout and the reaction of other countries, which played a larger role in the international media coverage than anything else. David assigned me to work on the coverage in Israel and the reaction of influencers there, while he worked with Team Netanyahu and Team Gantz on the appropriate political reception.

The media and think tanks that focus on the White House in general and Israeli-Palestinian issues more specifically are sophisticated, but in competition with social media they are increasingly pressed to make instantaneous responses to events. This would be difficult with such a comprehensive plan for a historically complicated region, so we aimed to provide enough of an overview to allow these thought leaders to see what was relevant to them and come out in favor, but without undercutting the White House rollout. The groups we briefed ranged from pro-Israel U.S. lobbying groups to small political parties in the Israeli Knesset that make the policy issues discussed in the plan their primary reason for being.

For me, one of these briefings involved some old-fashioned cloak-and-dagger techniques. Ambassador Friedman asked me to connect with a certain influential member of the Knesset and describe the plan to him personally. The catch was that if anyone saw us together right before the rollout, that member of the Knesset would be pressured to issue a public statement. I needed to convey the information discreetly so he wouldn't be compelled to say anything about the plan before it was released.

Compounding the problem was that this member of the Knesset was also a cabinet member, which meant that he had security and staff with him at all times. Rabbinic school does not train you for this type of challenge, so I used a friendly go-between to arrange a surreptitious meeting. The cabinet member was stuck at his ministry with all-night work, and the ministry was the last place I could be seen at that moment, but my friend was keen to orchestrate a spy-novel scenario.

He had me driven onto the ministry campus in an embassy car and dropped off in the far corner of the upper parking lot, after which the car left immediately. A black Mazda 3 series driven by my accomplice stopped at the corner, and I quickly hopped in and lay down on the back floor. The car pulled up to the front of the ministry building, where the cabinet minister jumped into the front. Our mutual friend then headed for the exit road, and we had about ten minutes to drive around before the cabinet member had to be back in the building or his security would get nervous. Still lying on the back floor, I explained the salient points of the Peace to Prosperity Vision, why it was coming out now, why this politician should persuade his caucus and followers to support the plan or at least not openly condemn it. He asked all the correct questions, clearly having done his homework. I am pleased to say that this meeting never leaked. When the plan rolled out publicly, this Knesset member and his caucus were temperate in their response, which was about as good as we could expect from them.

David and Jared engineered a way that both Prime Minister Netanyahu and General Gantz could be receptive to the plan, without undue meddling in Israeli politics. Remarkably, they were also able to secure agreement among Israeli elected leaders who collectively represented more than 75 percent of the Israeli people, during a never-ending election season, thanks to the equity that the administration had built up across the political spectrum. Coming out with the Vision in a first presidential term would reassure Israelis that the concerns they normally have about a second-term president with nothing to lose politically would not come up in the course of negotiations.

Man plans and God laughs. In normal times, the rollout of a comprehensive Middle East peace plan would be what everyone was talking about in the Beltway. But in the four days leading up to the launch of the Deal of the Century, the president's first impeachment trial was wrapping up, he received his first in-depth briefing on the emerging coronavirus pandemic, and the United Kingdom publicly committed to a 5G deal with the Chinese carrier company Huawei. There had been constant concern about a black swan event, because everything that could be thrown at President Trump was already thrown at him, and he seemed to be getting stronger, not weaker. Little was yet known about Covid-19, which threatened to be the challenge that could not be defeated.

The UK's decision to move forward with a Chinese company for its 5G network infrastructure was very disappointing. The UK is our closest ally, and President Trump felt that his own support for the Brexit movement was crucial to elevating Boris Johnson to the office of prime minister. Trump was exceedingly clear with all of our allies about the downgrading of intelligence sharing we would be forced to make if our allies used Chinese infrastructure in their 5G rollout, and getting this information when he was riding high raised his ire and immediately demanded ramifications. So the smooth ride into the rollout hit its first road bumps.

The biggest source of confusion among those participating in or observing the Peace to Prosperity plan was the question of Israel's ability to apply sovereignty to parts of Judea and Samaria. I was not privy to every conversation on the issue, but I do know that the peace team would have addressed it before the rollout had the White House not been confronting those other challenges at precisely this moment.

Another bump in the road, or so I thought, occurred in the wake of two meetings I attended late on the night of January 27. The first was with a leadership group from Judea and Samaria, invited by the prime minister, to be briefed on the Vision under strict confidentiality. The second meeting was with another member of the Samaria council, but someone whom the rest of the group did not like meeting or being associated with. My job was not to choose sides in a personality conflict, but to give a clear picture of what would be happening so that they as leaders and influencers could communicate effectively to their constituents. Both meetings went well, and while there were numerous disagreements with specific aspects of the Vision, the attendees agreed to be either positive or neutral in their public statements, remaining silent on points of disagreement out of respect for the relationship that the Trump administration had built over the previous three years.

I finally went to sleep at 2:30 a.m., knowing that the day ahead might be among the most significant of my professional life. My phone began to ring at 3:30. Apparently someone from the Judea and Samaria leadership group I had just met with, the mayor of a tiny town, decided to go on record with the Israeli press against the Vision. This was remarkable in multiple ways. First, it was a breach of the confidentiality agreement, which had been a condition for getting the briefing. Second, during the meeting this person had indicated that he was comfortable with the Vision, and his questions were not particularly probing. Finally, his statement to the press was made against the wishes of his colleagues who had attended the meeting with him.

I will not ascribe much importance to that person's statements because they did not move the needle for anyone above my level on the American side. But the violation of our confidentiality agreement was disappointing. What became clear to me later was that this person spoke to the press only because of a personality clash with another representative of the Jewish communities of Judea and Samaria. His criticism of the Vision was not a question of policy, but of internal politics. Over four years, I saw many leaders act in their own interest and not in the interest of the people who elected them, and this was just one example, but it was disappointing to me because this mayor of a tiny town went on the record with his criticism after being invited to the White House and having his questions answered by a member of the peace team. The chutzpah was shocking.

This kind of political gamesmanship should not have been surprising to me, but it was. When someone wishes to be a leader in a country's governance, I would expect that person to make sacrifices to protect its security. If you want to play dirty politics or settle a personal score when the issue is something like where to build a road, it won't be particularly damaging, but if you allow personality politics to intrude in an issue of national security or regional peace, you bring shame on yourself as a leader. If we expect young men and women in the armed forces to be willing to make the ultimate sacrifice in defense of their country, how can we not expect political leaders to put their personal ambitions and grievances aside for the safety and security of their country?

Unable to fall back asleep, I called everyone I knew who might pass a message back to the groups I had met with the previous evening, and gave a lecture on the difference between leadership and cowardice. Leadership in this case would have been playing by the agreed-upon rules, and then debating the particulars he objected to after he got back to Israel. Cowardice was preempting his hosts in disclosing pieces of a plan he didn't like, when it was clear to me that he didn't comprehend the plan in its entirety. In retrospect, however, my reaction to the mayor's statement was a mistake, because it elevated that opinion to a level it did not merit. As far as the White House was concerned, no one knew who the person was or cared what he said.

After I had finished my phone calls, I took an extra-long time on my morning prayer, had a big cup of coffee, and rolled out of the hotel at 7:15 wearing a new suit and tie, because it isn't every day that you might get to play a role in Middle East peace. I enjoyed the twelve-minute walk to the Eisenhower Executive Office Building, right next to the White House, as it gave me time to think and lay out my goals and priorities for the day. Once inside the building, I headed for Avi Berkowitz's office suite, which I expected to be ground zero for last-minute preparations. After checking my emails and making two phone calls with Israeli reporters, I realized that I was mistaken. I ran over to the West Wing of the White House and found that the action was happening there. Jared had a series of meetings and calls lined up, three to five minutes a shot. Avi, Cassidy, and the team from the National Security Council were making final tweaks to the Vision document, printing copies, and ensuring that everyone invited to the rollout felt like a VIP and was seated correctly.

There is always a great deal of pomp and circumstance at any ceremony in the White House, but every time I just walked into the building I got chills. I often felt like pinching myself. How could I be so lucky as to be able to work there and serve my country? I asked friends who worked for the State Department and for the National Security Council across administrations, "Does it ever lose its awesomeness? Can you ever walk in and think it's just another day at the job" Across the board, they all told me they still got a special feeling no matter how many times they had been there and no matter how hard the work. The fact that the Peace to Prosperity Vision was rolled out at the White House demonstrated the seriousness that the president was attaching to it.

The East Room was packed with the Who's Who of the U.S.-Israel relationship, including senators and representatives from Congress, cabinet members, faith-based leadership, and more. Yet other than the president of the United States and the prime minister of Israel, no one garnered more attention than three people sitting in the third row. They were the ambassadors to the United States from the United Arab Emirates, the Kingdom of Bahrain, and Oman. There were many rounds of applause throughout the day, but none came anywhere near the thunderous applause that these three ambassadors received. This reception from some of the most powerful and influential people in the United States was captured on live TV streamed around the world. The ambassadors had not come to the White House to endorse the Peace to Prosperity Vision. They had broad-stroke knowledge of it, but not specific details. They came in support of moving the ball forward in the region in practical ways that can also lead to a better future for the Palestinian people. It is impossible to overstate the courage it took for them to attend, and for the leaders of their countries to send them.

Middle East peace plans have always been met with great skepticism by the pro-Israel crowd, as well as by commonsense Americans who wonder why our government expends limited time and resources on a seemingly impossible challenge. Among people who had been watching the Middle East under President Trump, there was cautious optimism and a lot of confidence that the administration was on the right track. Yet at the same time, Trump was an outside-the-box president, and dozens of conversations I had had in the embassy in Jerusalem indicated a feeling that his actions to that point might be a buildup for strongarming Israel into major compromises down the road.

People knew that something was in the works, and because the Peace to Prosperity Vision was kept confidential until the rollout, it was the subject most asked about by visitors to the embassy, including members of Congress. Since David Friedman had become a cult hero for the right-leaning pro-Israel crowd, the greatest assurance I could give anyone concerned about it was that nothing would be released without his signoff. I also mentioned that David and Jared (as well as Greenblatt and Berkowitz) were in full agreement on the goals, and only rarely disagreed on methods. In fact, David always told people, publicly and privately, that he and Jared were in sync. This to me was a great example of teamwork, because it could have been easy to paint himself as the savior of the right, but he did not.

The Israeli-Palestinian conflict takes up a disproportionate amount of attention in the United States and around the world, and much energy is wasted on unrealistic goals and political posturing. The United States in the past has winked at unrealistic approaches, or even proposed them. As they became baked into expectations for the region, peace moved further away. Continuing to propose the same unachievable goals under different branding only does harm.

The Peace to Prosperity Vision is different. It is not a "Peace Plan" or a "Peace Initiative," because plans and initiatives set up processes and systems, which in this region are prone to be derailed, most often by terrorism and mayhem. It was not designed to initiate a process, but to reset expectations for what Middle East peace could realistically look like.

The administration knew that the Palestinians would have been unlikely to accept any peace deal, even on the very same terms they had demanded in the past. They simply were not in a frame of mind to accept any type of deal that was proposed, even one that met their narrative precisely. Certainly, they were not capable of coming to the table in January 2020 on the basis of the Peace to Prosperity Vision, and likely not in the next year or more. Through many years of negotiations and processes and UN resolutions, they had become more entrenched in unrealistic positions, such as dividing Jerusalem, or an unlimited right of return to Israel for self-defined Palestinian refugees. These were reinforced by international bodies and NGOs. Even if the Palestinians knew that these positions were not realistic, they couldn't retreat without losing face. Mahmoud Abbas, president of the Palestinian Authority, was now in the fourteenth year of his four-year presidential term and had an approval rating of under 20 percent (which has since gone lower). He had no popular mandate. He was an old man, and from his perspective, accepting the Vision would be capitulating to everything he had fought against for twenty-five years.

The Peace to Prosperity Vision did not set up a process of negotiation, but instead it set down a marker, presenting a realistic picture of a possible future for the region, and it offered a four-year window for Palestinians to think about buying in. Once a realistic plan for comprehensive peace was put forward, all previous plans and roadmaps could be relegated to the dustbin of history.

Prior to the rollout, a lot of very smart people pushed back on the Peace to Prosperity team. If there was no chance that the Palestinians would even engage, why spend the bandwidth of the White House on what appeared to be just an intellectual exercise or a vanity play? The decision to roll out the Vision in January 2020 was strategic. Even though it was clear that the Palestinians wouldn't agree or even engage at present, this step would begin the process of eliminating some macro issues that lingered over the region. First is the way that every decision in the Middle East is seen through the prism of the Israeli-Palestinian conflict. This has given the Palestinians a de facto veto on progress in the region until they walk away with a peace accord that is satisfactory to them. It has held back the Palestinian people on a micro level and has hampered the ability of countries to partner productively with Israel for their own betterment and regional improvement. Another macro issue is that the U.S. alliance with Israel is given faulty litmus tests, because the United States has to weigh every action it takes in the region according to how it looks through the Israel–Palestinian prism. One example is the stupidity of U.S. government planes not flying directly between our own allies in the region. These macro issues will not be gone immediately but will lose their grip, and with proper leadership they will eventually disappear forever.

While it was realistic, the Vision addressed many difficult questions that had not been discussed in any previous negotiations, such as final borders and final status of refugees. These had been regarded as issues on which no agreement could be reached at present, so there was no point in confronting them. The premise of past dealmakers had been to start with the easy stuff, spend time on confidence-building measures, and eventually you can tackle the hard issues. It sounds reasonable, but it didn't work. No amount of confidence-building measures will make it feasible for the State of Israel to divide Jerusalem, or make Israel comfortable with an unlimited right of return of self-defined Palestinian refugees to Israel, or a new Palestinian state. Conversely, it seems unlikely that confidence-building measures will ever induce the Palestinians writ large to welcome a state that is the homeland of the Jewish people anywhere within the boundaries of the current State of Israel. If we know these are intractable sticking points, what good does putting them off do?

In earlier peace processes, the two sides were to spend months or years in confidence-building measures, which if successful would prepare for compromises on the final status issues. The participants in the confidence-building exercises themselves knew that they were being set up for an impossible task, and that is why I was met with deafening silence when I first arrived at the embassy and asked for the names of the top twenty up-and-coming leaders on both sides who could forge ahead with opportunities for peace and integration. There are not twenty graduates of decades of U.S.-funded programs who are ready for the next step of leadership among the Palestinian people. There are many graduates of these programs, and almost all are invested in a formula that has not worked. They succeed in reinforcing prior assumptions, but have not cultivated leaders interested in rethinking the paradigm.

The Peace to Prosperity Vision took a new approach, setting out what was viewed as the only realistic goal, including all of the final status issues. With the goal clearly articulated, the confidence-building measures and processes to achieve it would be more purposeful. The Vision began with three principles that were not part of any prior negotiations or peace plans. The first is that the Palestinian Authority must develop mechanisms for rule of law and financial transparency. The United States should not have its fingerprints on the creation or approval of a state that does not establish basic human rights and clear rules for living under its authority, with fair processes of enforcement. The Palestinian Authority does not currently have a plan for setting out clear rules that protect the rights of all people living under its power. It defies reason why the international community, or at least the United States, would not require basic rule of law and protection of human rights as prerequisites for statehood. One important aspect of the rule of law is financial transparency. Today, major components of PA governance are run like a family-owned business, leading to a culture of cronyism and corruption. Too many Palestinians are dependent on the PA power structure, while the PA itself acts like a dependent of international organizations. The result is a dearth of ingenuity and self-reliance, and little progress for the Palestinian people since the PA was founded in 1994.

The Palestinian Authority could quickly raise GDP with a more transparent financial system and an open approach to integrating with the Israeli economy. After all, the government of Guatemala recognized the benefits of closer relations with Israel, despite being more than six thousand miles away and not having a similar culture or language. That is one reason why Guatemala opened an embassy in Jerusalem just two days after the United States did. Guatemala's ambassador to Israel, Mario Bacuro, emphasized one point in nearly every speech he made: Israel is the Startup Nation, producing more startups and job opportunities per capita than any other country on earth. Why wouldn't Guatemala want to be a beneficiary of the economic boon that the Israeli market brings? The Palestinians have much more in common with Israelis, besides being their neighbors, yet their leaders refuse to make the necessary steps to gain the economic benefits of cooperation with Israel.

The United States is not going to be more pro-Palestinian than the Palestinians. It is up to the Palestinian Authority to demonstrate that they can be leaders for their own people if they are to become partners for peace.

The second basic principle of the Vision is simple: Do no harm. This requires acknowledging realities on the ground, which is more difficult than imagining how things might be. It is easy to sit in the ivory towers or the halls of the European Union or the State Department and tell the Middle East how it should be. I cannot say what the ideal situation in the Middle East would be. That is an academic exercise, or wishful dreaming. The Vision puts a priority on the security of the entire area from the Mediterranean Sea to the Jordan River and from Lebanon and Syria down to Egypt, and in doing so it starts with recognizing some essential facts. It's clear that only one force is qualified to bring security to what is today Israel and the Israeli-controlled territories, and that is Israel itself. We have seen the reality of what happens when Israel retreats, as demonstrated in Gaza and southern Lebanon. The world praised Israel for those decisions, and promised support if those risks for the sake of peace ever came back to bite Israel. Yet the goodwill generated by the Israeli retreat—some would say surrender—had already evaporated within weeks when the vacuum was filled by terrorists bent on Israel's destruction.

The case of Lebanon, and the rearming of Hezbollah under the watchful but ineffectual eye of the United Nations Disengagement Observer Force, shows that Israel cannot trust the international community for security. The Gaza disengagement of 2005 demonstrates that Israel cannot trust the Palestinians to control their own territory in a way that keeps Israelis safe. The only other power that Israelis would trust to provide security in this part of the Middle East is the United States. On the other hand, a fundamental principle of the State of Israel is that it protects itself by itself. An Israeli-Palestinian peace arrangement based on U.S. troops might sound good from a certain perspective, but it would be destined to fail because those against peace in the region would make U.S. soldiers their primary target, which would understandably diminish the relationship between the United States and Israel. And it most certainly would not be in the interest of the United States, or of Israel, for U.S. soldiers to be tasked with a permanent peacekeeping mission in the region.

So the only entity that can and should secure the entire area of what will be a Palestinian State and the State of Israel is the defense forces of Israel. The Israel Defense Forces comprise some of the most highly trained and capable military forces in the world. They have been tried and tested in one of the most challenging neighborhoods in the world. The IDF is a citizen army and probably the most unifying organization across Israeli society. It is not perfect—no organization is—but it does the most effective job of keeping Israelis safe.

The Peace to Prosperity Vision recognizes the Israel Defense Forces as the necessary means of providing security in the entire area. It appropriately calls for Israeli security control over Gaza as well, since Israelis cannot contemplate going forward with peace when they are under constant threat of a rocket barrage.

The third basic principle of the Vision caught nearly everyone by surprise, but frankly it's appalling that anyone thought it controversial: People should not be forced to leave their homes. This does not mean that everywhere a Jewish house is now located will be part of sovereign Israel and everywhere a Palestinian home now stands will be in sovereign Palestine. It means that *most* Jewish homes in Judea and Samaria—the disputed West Bank—will be part of Israel, and *many* Palestinian homes in these territories will be part of a future State of Palestine. But neither Israel nor a State of Palestine will be ethnically cleansed.

For Israelis, this is a given. In Israel there are Jews, Muslims, Christians, Druze, Bahai, and others who are full citizens with equal rights. There are Muslim members of the Knesset and the Supreme Court. There are Muslims and Christians holding high rank in the IDF, serving as chief medical officers in major hospitals, and the like. Yet it had been widely thought that any future Palestinian state would have the right to be *Judenrein*, free of Jews. I don't know where this concept originated, but it has become so entrenched in expectations for the region that there are dozens of organizations whose entire reason for existing is to report on the building of houses by Jews in Judea and Samaria. The reason is that every Jewish home built is viewed as another obstacle to a future Palestinian state. Imagine if Israelis felt that every new Arab home or Christian church in Israel spelled doom for the Jewish homeland. This of course is preposterous. People of many other ethnic and religious backgrounds contribute to the fabric of Israeli society and make the country better.

Admittedly, these principles are difficult pills for the Palestinians to swallow. In this book I have blamed the Palestinian narrative for thwarting peace and progress. But to be fair, the Palestinians are like any other interest group in that they will take whatever they are able to get, and for far too long the international community has held them to a very different standard from others, especially the Israelis. Since the Oslo Accords, the Palestinians have been treated as the underdogs that much of the liberal world wants to root for. Terrorists who kill Israelis are excused as freedom fighters, and the payments to their families are winked at. Shooting rockets from kindergartens in Gaza toward kindergartens in Israel is excused on the ground that you can't expect better from people living in a so-called "open-air prison." Human rights violations too numerous to count, but evidently not important enough for NGOs to report on consistently, are forgiven because of the Israeli "occupation." For the same reason, cronyism, financial crimes, and a four-year presidential term stretching to fourteen years and beyond are not matters of concern. With all this indulgence, it's no wonder that the Palestinian leaders have become more strident in their demands.

But there is a growing disconnect between the Palestinian leadership and the Palestinian people. For one thing, the majority of Palestinians are under the age of thirty, while the average Palestinian leader is over seventy-five. Young Palestinians have seen Israel thrive as the Startup Nation, and have seen cousins and friends, Israeli Arabs, choose to participate in the opportunities it offers. The internet and social media have opened their eyes to opportunities in other countries too. This isn't to discount their aspirations for nationhood, but many young Palestinians are more interested in charting a better future for themselves than in fighting the same war their parents and grandparents fought, in the same way.

While the Palestinians are held back by their own leadership, Israel has moved forward rapidly, becoming a technological powerhouse creating more jobs and industries than any other country of its size, and more than many countries multiple times its size. Israel is now older than half the countries in the United Nations. Its core systems—judicial, security, financial—are far from perfect but generally work well and promote equality of opportunity for all citizens. This has been accomplished in spite of wars, intifadas, rocket attacks, threats from Iran, condemnation at the UN, and a divided parliamentary system. To repeat what Senator Lindsey Graham often says, "Israel has the nicest house in a pretty rough neighborhood."

Yet the international community's approach to the region has been either: a) Israel is the problem, or b) if you solve the Israeli-Palestinian conflict you will solve the other Middle East challenges. The Trump administration took the opposite approach: b) If you solve the Israeli-Palestinian conflict, you have done something fantastic, but it won't change the Middle East writ large; and a) Israel is not the source of the problem, it is the source of solutions, and the countries that don't recognize this and act on it are only hurting themselves. This realization has not yet dawned on the Palestinian leadership, but eventually it will. The Palestinian people need and deserve a better life, and they will not get it through the negotiating points first set out twenty-five years ago.

24

REALISM AND CLARITY

I n the middle of a contentious election cycle that never seemed to end, Benjamin Netanyahu became the first Israeli prime minister to hold up a map showing the conceptual outline of a future Palestinian state. That was an act of great political courage. Many of Netanyahu's supporters in Israel were not interested in the language of the Peace to Prosperity Vision. Once they heard the term "Palestinian state," everything else became irrelevant. Before castigating that response as a sign of belligerence, we need to understand what Israelis have witnessed and lived through since the Oslo Accords. A leftist government and a population that leaned left of center had dreamed of a Palestinian state existing side by side with Israel. Those dreams, embodied in the Oslo Process, resulted in thousands of terror victims and an actual terror state, Gaza, bordering Israel and able to direct rockets at more than half its population on a moment's notice. All this moved the Israeli population rightward politically. For many, the mere mention of a Palestinian state by the people elected to steer clear of that perceived danger was shocking. But Netanyahu knew that the Vision was likely to be the only opportunity in a generation to break through the Palestinian veto. This courageous decision may have been politically costly to him.

Contrast the response of Mahmoud Abbas, president of the Palestinian Authority. For more than two and a half years, while the Vision was being formulated, the peace team repeatedly encouraged Abbas to meet with them and share his thoughts and plans. He refused to do so. When the Vision was released, Abbas could have claimed a victory as the first Palestinian leader to get Israel to agree publicly to a map of a future State of Palestine. He could have said he agreed with ten points but disagreed with thirty. He could have pronounced the plan not as bad as the PA had expected. He could have taken a number of different approaches other than wholesale rejection. But once again, he didn't miss an opportunity to miss an opportunity.

Rather than engage on aspects of the plan, the PA went back to the tried-and-true playbook, running to the United Nations to decry the Vision and try to rouse international condemnation of it. Abbas took the conceptual map for a Palestinian state—the first one that a prime minister of Israel had received as realistic—and proceeded to complain about how terrible it was. But the map had not been put forward by Israel; it was created by the U.S. government. Israel had only agreed to negotiate with the Palestinians on the basis of the Peace to Prosperity Vision, including the conceptual map. So instead of seeking the usual anti-Israel condemnations at the UN, the PA and its friends were forced to decide if they wanted to condemn the United States.

The UN General Assembly did condemn the Peace to Prosperity Vision, but the Security Council—which had fully abandoned Israel in December 2016 with Resolution 2334—didn't even propose a resolution rejecting it. That was a watershed moment. Numerous Arab and Muslim countries put out friendly statements regarding the Vision and its new way of looking at the region and the Israeli-Palestinian conflict.

There were several reasons for the lack of international objection to the Peace to Prosperity Vision. One is that its unveiling had been prepared by a top-to-bottom approach to diplomacy fashioned in the image of a president who was not afraid to challenge traditional norms. It began with Ambassador Nikki Haley arriving at the UN and explaining to the international community that the United States would not be the bank of the world when other countries need money, but also the whipping child in international forums when other governments wish to deflect blame for their own domestic problems. The United States would be keeping track of who votes for what, and why. And it would stand up consistently for our ally Israel at the UN, and against the double standard applied to Israel versus every other country. At the same time, the United States expected our friends and allies to have our back, not just behind closed doors, but publicly and clearly.

Second, when the Vision was finally unveiled, leaders around the world were relieved to see that it was realistic. It started from facts on the ground and then described what could plausibly be achieved. Israel would cede the territory for creating a new state, but the Palestinians would first need to demonstrate the capability to govern a state. The last thing the Middle East and the world need is another failed state. If a new state is going to be created, it must rest upon a full and transparent set of governing laws.

Third, the peace team anticipated that the Palestinians would run around the world trying to discredit the Vision any way they could, so a four-year window was provided for opting in to negotiate from its premises. This gave the Palestinians time to weigh the benefits and costs. During that time, they might come around to accepting that a realistic approach was the only way forward.

Fourth, the Vision gave reassurance to Israelis by contemplating that Israel would be able to apply sovereignty over parts of Judea and Samaria, with the support of the United States. There was debate among the peace team about the timing and manner of applying sovereignty, which led to confusion between the team and Israel, and within the Israeli government as well. It made for wonderful tabloid fodder, but this one area of confusion, lasting for about a week, was only a small bump in the otherwise cohesive rollout of a complicated, historic plan. For the sake of future U.S. policy, it is important to be clear about the benefits of applying sovereignty.

In the Middle East, any lack of clarity leads to confusion, chaos, and violence, as demonstrated in the Arab Spring, for example. The nebulous legal status of Jewish homes in the West Bank (Judea and Samaria) has resulted in countless challenges and disputes. The central issue here is not whether Jews should or should not be able to live in their biblical homeland, though I believe they should. The question is about national policy and what happens when policy decisions are not consistent with the national interest. The reality is that Israelis cannot live safely within the pre-1967 borders. It is not in Israel's national interest to return to those borders, nor is it in the interest of the United States for Israel to return to indefensible borders.

These realities must be the premises for bringing greater clarity to the West Bank.

As long as Israel does not actively apply its own sovereignty over its own areas, it is possible to think that the Israeli presence in the West Bank may be temporary. The legal ambiguity feeds the narrative that Jews are now an aberration in their ancient homeland, and it creates a vacuum that violent forces can fill. If Israel were to apply sovereignty over parts of Judea and Samaria, it would bring clarity to both Israelis and Palestinians living there. In the Peace to Prosperity Vision, the United States would recognize Israeli sovereignty over parts of the West Bank, while Israel in return would freeze building in areas that could be part of a State of Palestine as outlined in the agreed-upon conceptual map. But Israel should not need to wait for a non-state entity to decide it wants to pursue a realistic peace before Israel can apply sovereignty.

Moreover, the United States should not be supporting the creation of a *Judenrein* state in the West Bank, just as it should not support any state that discriminates against any ethnic or religious group. If Palestinians regard the very presence of Jews in their vicinity as an insurmountable obstacle to peace, let's just admit that peace in the region will not happen.

The Palestinians under their current leadership will not accept the Vision, but the four-year window for opting in would give them time to move past their rejectionism and see what the Vision offers for their own betterment. Other countries also have time to evaluate the plan. Meanwhile, Israel could choose the application of sovereignty, the world would keep turning, and Israel would be recognized for taking a risk by agreeing to a conceptual map of a Palestinian state. It is rather telling that the Palestinian leadership adopted a strategy of "hope Trump loses," which essentially means they wanted a status quo that serves only themselves and not their people.

25

EVEN IN A PANDEMIC

The rollout of the Peace to Prosperity Vision in January 2020 was supposed to be the featured story of the year. It was the featured story for about two weeks, during which it received a fair hearing from the international community as well as some open-minded journalists. While not universally praised, it was not dead on arrival either, as so many pundits had predicted.

Miles Davis famously said, "Time isn't the main thing, it's the only thing." When the Peace to Prosperity Vision was launched, the president was leading the United States with as much momentum as he had had throughout his presidency. As David Friedman enjoyed pointing out, if you went to sleep on January 1, 2017, and woke up on January 1, 2020, you would be thrilled with the metrics for the United States. Record employment, strong trade. No new military engagements, lower taxes, and a criminal justice reform act that passed Congress in a broad bipartisan fashion. Those of us working on the Vision all felt that nothing short of a black swan event would derail a second term, even if the polling was not encouraging. Among senior advisors to the president it was far from unanimous that he was on a glidepath to reelection, but the peace team were confident.

Covid-19 was more than a black swan, it was a once-in-a-century pandemic that touched every single part of the world and caused widespread fear and concern. Supply chains crumbled and much-needed medical supplies and personal protective equipment were too often unobtainable. Americans were stranded across the four corners of the globe. The Peace to Prosperity Vision was not on anyone's priority list.

I am sure you remember the first several weeks of Covid chaos, and "two weeks to flatten the curve," and videos of the public cheering and applauding medical personnel at their change of shift every night in appreciation for their heroic work. The White House summoned all the power and resources of the United States and in record time repatriated over one million Americans from too many countries to count; set up manufacturing so that not a single American who needed a respirator would be without one; and challenged the pharmaceutical industry to get vaccines and therapeutics through the approval process faster than ever before. Soon, personal protective equipment became more readily available to medical workers across the country. Secretary Mnuchin led in getting the Coronavirus Aid, Relief, and Economic Security (CARES) Act passed into law and implemented. It is impossible to overstate how consequential this one act was; it may possibly have saved the global economy.

During those stressful times, I witnessed exemplary leadership in many places, and I saw that it had two defining characteristics. The first was readjusting the lens of leadership to focus primarily on your country's own citizenry. To protect and care for your citizens is an obligation of national leadership. Second, once the urgent needs of one's own citizens were being addressed, there was outreach to friends and allies. Just as the Covid-19 virus knows no boundaries, fighting it required international cooperation. There were daily calls between the United States and Israel to share data, best practices, and technology. That sharing of information saved thousands of lives.

During the darkest early days of the pandemic, there was great confidence that vaccines and therapeutics were overwhelmingly likely to come from the United States and Israel. This confidence was not exclusively expressed by Americans or Israelis. I heard it personally from countless diplomats as well as leaders of major corporations. There is a common gene in the makeup of the United States and Israel that encourages outside-the-box thinking, which can yield breakthroughs in short periods of time.

Covid-19 is a horrendous pandemic whose effects on the world will be ongoing for many years. One consequence that appeared quickly was a humbling and centering effect on leaders and citizens alike. People asked themselves: What really matters? What will our legacies be? While medical professionals risk their lives to care for strangers, what can the rest of us do to make our part of the world a better place?

Still, in these circumstances, peace between the Israelis and the Palestinians seemed like a rich person's problem. When you are focused on dealing with extraordinary challenges at home, there's little energy left for outside issues that seem less pressing. Yet as the Israeli government focused most of its attention on fighting the pandemic, there was also an awareness that the clock was running out on the Trump administration. Whatever Trump's odds of winning reelection were in January 2020, by May or June those odds had plummeted. The Israeli government led by Netanyahu felt a responsibility to maximize cooperation with the United States while the two countries enjoyed the closest relationship they ever had.

Secretary Pompeo made his first international trip in the Covid era on May 13. At the time, face-to-face meetings were being kept to a minimum, with only small numbers of people, but diplomacy needed to continue. Pompeo went to Israel, and one reason was to meet with Ambassador Friedman. After Pompeo's plane had taken off, Friedman called me to say he wasn't feeling well. I told him to call the embassy medical team and they sprang into action, arriving at the ambassador's home in full hazmat gear to administer a Covid test, which came back negative. Still, the medical professionals, along with Pompeo and the prime minister, decided that Friedman should not participate in any of the meetings during this trip.

David phoned me and said, "I'm calling in the lefty from the bullpen. You have to attend the meetings for me." Normally I would have jumped at such an opportunity, but this time I was hesitant. I was sure that Pompeo would be disappointed not to see the ambassador, and I was certain that when Pompeo and Netanyahu met, they would not keep me in the room. Nevertheless, I asked David to call both of them and let them know I would be joining the meetings in his place.

Pompeo's plane would be the only one carrying non-Israelis to land in Israel that month, so its arrival would be noticed and eyes in the region were going to be laser-focused on his visit. Understanding the magnitude of the moment, I called David again to confirm that he had made the calls. He had conveyed the message to Pompeo, he told me, but when he spoke with Netanyahu the topic didn't come up. I was aghast. How was it possible that the whole point of calling didn't come up in the conversation? Friedman responded, "I called the prime minister and he immediately said, 'David, I hear you aren't feeling well,' and so I replied, 'I'm feeling fine now, but the Covid test was the worst thing I've ever felt. They went so far into my nose it felt like she was trying to get brain matter for the test. It was terrible, just terrible!'" Friedman continued to complain about the Covid test for another two minutes until the prime minister cut him off and said, "David, you know I've been shot a few times, right?" It was one of the funniest lines he ever heard, Friedman told me, and that's why he forgot to tell the prime minister that I would attend the meetings in his stead.

Before Pompeo's arrival, everyone from the embassy had questions and concerns: Would he ask me to ride with him to Jerusalem? Would he be upset that the ambassador wasn't there? I had confidence that the visit would go well, though I resigned myself to the likelihood that I would be on the sidelines for most of it. Another concern of the embassy staff was: Would Pompeo be wearing a face mask? When he descended the steps of the plane wearing an awesome American flag mask, the whole embassy team breathed a sigh of relief.

I went to greet him at the red carpet, and we did one of those awkward elbow bumps. "The ambassador is very sorry not to be joining you," I said, "but he wants to protect you and the prime minister from getting sick." Pompeo replied, "I am pleased you will be joining me today." I took that to be a positive sign, and a little presumptuously I started walking toward the secretary's limo (an armored Suburban) thinking I would ride with him to Jerusalem. Apparently that wasn't the plan. His security politely guided me to the staff van that would follow in the motorcade. Of course I was deflated, and I could almost feel the disappointment of the embassy staff too. While it would have been unprecedented for a senior advisor to join the secretary of state in the ride to Jerusalem, our embassy had gotten used to doing things a bit differently, and I could tell that my colleagues had been rooting for me. I know this seems like a funny point to focus on, but the microscopes were out on the trip. Already there were questions about why Friedman wasn't there, and speculation that maybe the embassy was being sidelined.

As it turned out, riding in the staff van was a great experience. I had the pleasure of sitting next to my good friend Morgan Ortagus, the spokesperson for the State Department. She told me that she and her husband were expecting a baby girl, and in that moment I could not have been happier for anyone. In the fast-moving world of diplomacy, you can sometimes forget that your colleagues have personal lives, and the look on Morgan's face as we pulled into Jerusalem, the holy city, was everything.

At the embassy, Pompeo invited me to discuss his agenda for the visit. In the course of our conversation, it became clear that Friedman had reassured him that I would be able to represent him well at the meetings and that I had his confidence. We went to the prime minister's home for public statements, followed by a three-hour meeting that covered a myriad of issues. Three things that happened in the meeting stand out in my memory.

First, Netanyahu wanted to be sure that Pompeo was comfortable with the group around the table for high-level discussion, and I knew it was a polite way of asking if Pompeo was okay with having me there in Friedman's absence. Pompeo put his arm around the back of my chair and told the prime minister that he was very comfortable with the team he had there. I am positive that I had a silly grin on my face for the rest of the day.

Second, when Pompeo and Netanyahu spoke about the International Criminal Court, I was surprised at how fluent Pompeo was in every nuance of every issue that the prime minister brought up. But I shouldn't have been. From the moment I told him I knew Adam from Wichita, up to a conversation we had about infrastructure the previous week, Pompeo had always known more than I did about the subject at hand. I am truly concerned about what would happen if we started discussing the Talmud.

Third, when Pompeo and Netanyahu talked about Iran, they didn't speak only as Israelis or Americans, but as the last defense of the West against unchecked terror-supporting mullahs in Tehran. They were united in purpose, and the clock of the Trump administration seemed to be ticking as the meeting went on.

Afterward, Pompeo went back to the embassy for meetings with the defense minister, Benny Gantz, and the foreign minister, Gabi Ashkenazy. Both meetings went well, though the disconnect between those two on one end and Netanyahu on the other seemed unbridgeable. After these back-to-back meetings, Pompeo wryly asked me, "Do they think I'm a marriage counselor?" Israel appeared to have a unity government in name only.

After those meetings I had the honor of presenting the U.S. flag that flew over the embassy in Jerusalem to Pompeo on the ambassador's behalf. While only ten people were present at the ceremony, Pompeo was clearly touched. Then I asked him to join me in presenting a flag to Morgan Ortagus. Morgan personified the incredible extra effort that team members put in to make the secretary of state successful, and she proved to be a valuable link in keeping our embassy in step with Pompeo and his team. As I walked down the stairs with Pompeo toward his limo, he put his hand on my back and said, "Lightstone, ride with me." I am sure that jumping into the air and doing a fist pump was not the most mature way to respond to such an invitation, but they don't come along every day. As I basically ran to the other side of the limo, I noticed that the entire embassy security team were giving me a thumbs-up.

Pompeo's visit was highly successful. His very first trip abroad as secretary of state was to Israel, and now his first trip during the Covid-19 pandemic was to Israel. The message was clear: The United States will stand with Israel at all times, and whether you are the president of the Palestinian Authority or a mullah

in Iran or even a bureaucrat in Israel looking at Chinese investment, the United States under the foreign policy leadership of
its chief diplomat would continue to be engaged and involved,
even in a pandemic.

26

A TIME FOR CHOOSING

I f Ambassador Friedman had been present in the meetings with Secretary Pompeo, the application of Israeli sovereignty over select parts of Judea and Samaria would have been the main topic of discussion, but the visit did at least put the subject back on the agenda. July 1 had come to be seen as the deadline for Israel to make this move. I believe that the specific date originated in a misquote from an interview that Friedman gave in May, yet it made sense. If Israel was going to have the backing of the United States on the decision, there was a narrow window of opportunity because of U.S. domestic considerations. The president would be in full campaign mode by August, and an America First president shouldn't be bogged down in the nuances of sovereignty over a small piece of land in the Middle East that many Americans who supported him believe is part of Israel anyway. Some who opposed the application of sovereignty painted this maneuver as a political gift to Trump, thinking it would somehow boost his base even more, yet he was already batting 1000 to those who vote with Israel as a primary concern. On the other hand, introducing the concept of a Palestinian state and somehow dividing the biblical land of Israel could have cost support with those voters.

President Trump and his team were not motivated by politics, but wanted to create the correct policy whenever the right time arose.

For the government of Israel, the time for making some pretty important decisions appeared to be running short. I will not divulge any internal Israeli government conversations, but to describe them as combative may be an understatement.

Against this backdrop, on June 12, the ambassador from the United Arab Emirates to the United States published an open letter to the people of Israel in a popular Israeli daily, *Yediot Ahronoth*. This was the first public op-ed by a senior Gulf diplomat to appear in an Israeli newspaper. Ambassador Yousef Al Otaiba spoke directly to the people of Israel about opportunities for the UAE and Israel to become closer, while also expressing the view that a unilateral decision by Israel to move forward with what he called annexation in the West Bank would be detrimental to that purpose. Even so, the ambassador's openness about the mutual interest in enhancing the UAE-Israel relationship was important.

The UAE ambassador's open letter reflected the warming of relations in the region that Netanyahu had touted in his very first meetings with Kushner and Friedman. He called it the outside-in approach to fostering peace in the region. Peace can be had with other Arab states before it is possible with the Palestinians, and as those outside relationships warm up, the whole region will be better prepared to address the Palestinian issue. Relationships between Israel and Arab states began improving considerably when the United States under President Obama started leaning toward Iran and the Muslim Brotherhood. Those in the region who understood that these are two existential threats to peace and prosperity began working together behind the scenes to keep the region safe.

Ambassador Al Otaiba could have engaged publicly with the Israelis at any time over the previous few years, but the timing of this letter was clearly driven by the perceived July 1 deadline for applying sovereignty in Judea and Samaria. His message was that Israel had to choose between that action and a continued warming of relations with the GCC countries. The application of sovereignty would slow the trend toward normalization that had been growing steadily for months and even years, or possibly knock it off course for the foreseeable future.

For the Israelis, it was a time for choosing. The application of sovereignty was a substantive, achievable goal. If they chose to suspend this decision, they would need to receive more in return than just the continuation of an ongoing process of normalization. They would need a real and immediate peace. The time for discussion and analysis was over. A significant change in the status quo was now certain to occur; the question was what that change would be.

Friedman and I spent at least one hundred hours poring over maps showing more than fifty different permutations of what the West Bank could look like in various stages of the application of sovereignty, from one small area, through incremental steps, possibly all the way to a final settlement between Israelis and Palestinians. We tried to consider the question of Israeli sovereignty from every possible perspective. Meanwhile, Netanyahu and his team were going through the same process and contemplating incredibly weighty decisions. During the month of June, I spent countless hours embedded with the Israeli National Security Council team. We analyzed every conceivable decision tree and every possible outcome. We prepared numerous quality-of-life opportunities that Israel could offer the Palestinians, carefully weighing the security risks involved.

As the end of June approached, Friedman thought it was time to brief the president personally on the situation in Israel. In an unprecedented move, the State Department sent a military jet to bring the ambassador to the White House, along with David Milstein and me. It was an honor to fly on what is fondly called "milair" to Washington by way of Ramstein Air Base in Germany. Every interaction I had with U.S. military personnel was a positive experience and made me feel more patriotic. When the plane pulled into the refueling spot at Ramstein, two service members stood at attention. Friedman asked me why they were standing there like that, and I replied, "They are there to salute you, sir." Indeed, they were. Before we departed, the ambassador gave a U.S. Embassy Jerusalem challenge coin to everyone we interacted with at Ramstein.

In Washington we were picked up by State Department vehicles with a security team, which is not something normally done for U.S. ambassadors returning to the United States. But Friedman was pretty high profile, his reason for traveling was known, and with Black Lives Matter protestors in and around D.C., the State Department thought it would be prudent to provide him with a security detail. This worked out great for me, as it simplified the logistics of getting around.

There were rapid-fire meetings with the National Security team, Kushner, Pompeo, and others. At each meeting, Friedman gave a concise account of the situation in the Israeli government, how the unity government was and was not working, and where the relevant leaders and parties stood on the specific issue of the Peace to Prosperity Vision and the application of sovereignty. He concluded with a brief description of the personalities involved, and his recommendation for the next steps in the region. While everyone else in Washington had many items on their agenda, this was Friedman's sole focus, and he had spent a great many hours in discussions with Israel's prime minister, defense minister, foreign minister, and Speaker of the Knesset. He was the subject matter expert on the Peace to Prosperity Vision.

There were many reasons for the United States not to support an Israeli application of sovereignty over parts of Judea and
Samaria. For one thing, it was politically inconvenient. The president was fighting on all fronts and did not need another reason
for the international community to rally against him. He and
some of his advisors could see Operation Warp Speed coming to
fruition in developing Covid vaccines, even if some pundits were
already framing it in the context of the upcoming presidential
election and were at the same time accusing the president of
playing politics with the pandemic response and blaming him
for poor outcomes in the crisis. With all of this going on, it was
not the time to be opening another front to fight on.

Yet two persuasive arguments helped carry the day. The first
was that the United States had made a commitment to Israel and
should honor its commitment. Second, it made sense to continue
making progress in the region based on the Peace to Prosperity
Vision even if it made some people uncomfortable. If Israel did
not move forward in the Vision, there was no compelling reason
for the Palestinians to engage. In that case, what looked like the
most realistic opportunity for substantive change in the region
just two months earlier would go back in the drawer, possibly
forever.

We felt that if Pompeo, Friedman, and Kushner were aligned
on an issue, it was likely to receive the president's approval. We
got an allotted time to meet in the Oval Office to brief him personally. This was to be my first professional meeting there. I had
been with the president numerous times but never in a formal
sit-down meeting. I was comforted to know that I was likely to
be a silent observer, as the group would include the president's
chief of staff, Mark Meadows, along with Avi Berkowitz, Robert
O'Brien, Scott Leith. Kushner, Friedman, Pompeo, and others.
My role was to present a flag to the president, the very first one

to fly over the U.S. Embassy in Jerusalem, to thank him for his leadership on behalf of the embassy.

There was nervous anticipation as ten of us huddled in Jared's office prior to the meeting. It was probably the highest number of people we had gathered in one office in five months. The tension of Covid testing was still in the air, and it was a blistering day in Washington besides. I recall the comradery and confidence among the group, all working as a team with a clear purpose. I also remember feeling terrified walking into the most important room in the world. There wasn't much I needed to do, but I was still nervous. The others may have been nervous, but more likely inspired and a bit awestruck. To a person, they understood the importance of the mission, and also the awesomeness of the Oval Office.

Jared was extremely kind and arranged for the White House photographer to take pictures of me presenting the flag to the president. We were all shown into the Oval Office, and you could feel the excitement in the air. I kept fidgeting with my tie and lapel pin. Jared was called to see the president in the waiting room. Three minutes later he returned and motioned to me to give the flag to Friedman for the presentation. For a moment I was crushed, but when the president walked in thirty seconds later, it made sense. Trump's usual affable demeanor was replaced with a frown. We all jumped out of our seats as he entered, and another thing I noticed was how tall he is. I've been at events with him and even have a selfie with him, but as he took his long strides into the Oval Office, he looked about eight feet tall. Seeing the official photographer, he politely suggested that she was not needed for this meeting. I wondered if I should follow her out of the room, and tried to make eye contact with Jared for guidance. He signaled to me that I should stay.

What followed was thirty-five of the most memorable minutes

I have ever had. Unfortunately, I had seated myself on the yellow couch right behind the main principals, and I soon regretted it. The couch was as close to the president as you could be, but I had to turn awkwardly to see around Friedman in front of me, and every time I shifted position on the couch, Scott Leith, who was sitting next to me, had to shift too.

The president was not in a great mood and was not particularly moved by the presentation of the flag from the embassy. He was, however, able to go around the room in rapid fire and note what each person there was working on, what the progress was, and why it was or was not to his satisfaction. He may have gone through twenty major issues, and his grasp on who was doing what was impressive to me, at least in retrospect.

At the time, I was trying to melt into the couch. I knew the president would eventually look at me and say something, and I had no idea what it might be. He looked at me and named three things that Ambassador Friedman should be doing, in his opinion, and said, "Make sure it gets done. I'm sure it will. David is the best lawyer in all of America, but make sure it gets done." I felt as though I had won the first round of Russian roulette. The next fifteen minutes went by in a blur. The president understood the nuances of the Israeli unity government, the difference between annexation and application of sovereignty, and Judea and Samaria versus the West Bank. But his mood did not improve.

As the meeting ended. Pompeo, Kushner, and Friedman did a quick postmortem. It was obvious that we would need to fly back to Israel and put more elbow grease into perfecting the options on the table. Jared asked Avi Berkowitz and Scott Leith to come along with us. This was exciting for all of us because Israel hadn't had visitors other than Pompeo since Covid started, and it would demonstrate seriousness to the broader world if Avi and Scott were coming over from the White House.

27

SOMETHING BIGGER

After a brief quarantine and PCR tests in Israel, we went to the Prime Minister's Office. Scott Leith and I spent another twenty hours with the Israeli National Security team that week. Ambassador Friedman, Avi Berkowitz, and I met with the prime minister daily. We were aware that time was slipping away. I grew to appreciate how Scott was always on point, avoiding any personal or political commentary. David's remarkable relationship with the prime minister and Avi's prestige from the White House made our mission in Jerusalem the highest priority of the Israeli government, aside from its ongoing battle against Covid-19.

During the intense daily meetings on the upper floor of the Prime Minister's Office, Scott and Avi had an opportunity to meet with my friend Maoz. This was a turning point, as Avi and Maoz would become two of the primary players in the Abraham Accords. On Avi's last night in Israel before his return to the White House, we all went to dinner at Kazan in Raanana, Israel. I invited Maoz, Paul Packer, and Yariv, our friend from Morocco, to the dinner, as I felt it would be a relaxed atmosphere to explore any outside-the-box opportunities that the Peace to Prosperity Vision presented. After four exhausting days, the delicious meal was reinvigorating, and we were bouncing countless ideas from the sublime to the ridiculous off each other.

Seven weeks earlier, the Etihad flight carrying Covid relief supplies had been rejected by the Palestinian Authority because it landed in Israel first. Maoz and I were working on the possibility of direct flights from the UAE to Israel and special religious tourism visas, and we both felt that a breakthrough was achievable, but the White House would need to push hard on it. Over the previous eight months, I had cultivated a few select contacts from the UAE, Bahrain, Morocco, and Kosovo who communicated through me to Friedman, Kushner, and Berkowitz. I was convinced that Morocco would be the first of these countries to start offering flights to Israel for religious tourism, but it was clear that my interlocutors and I were all dealing with incomplete information.

Jared and Avi were in constant dialogue with the leadership from key countries in the Middle East and North Africa region. These conversations ranged across a broad spectrum of topics, but always circled back to the vision for peace. Maoz and Paul regaled the table with accounts of their travels in various countries and explained what those countries would be seeking from the United States and Israel in order to bring peace closer to the region. While I was pushing for direct flights as a priority, I now saw that there could be an opportunity for something bigger than a one-off bilateral deal on commercial flights. Even in the heat of July, with President Trump underwater in the polls, Israel with a frayed unity government, and the Peace to Prosperity team pulled in various directions, we were talking about exponential change and not just incremental steps.

That evening, Avi returned to Washington to report back to the White House. David Friedman is not one to leave anything on the table, so the very next morning I was at his home discussing the ten top achievable goals if we indeed had only five months left. Number two on that list was welcoming the first direct flight from the UAE to Israel on the special religious tourism idea that I convinced myself was possible.

Just hours later I received a phone call from Avi, who was in Newark waiting for his flight to Reagan National Airport. He had gotten a phone call from Yousef Al Otaiba, the UAE ambassador to the United States, saying they must meet urgently. Avi's tone of voice told me clearly that he couldn't wait to connect with Al Otaiba. Two days later, Avi called me to say there was an opportunity to do something much more consequential than I was hoping for, or had even imagined. He gave no more details, but I had never before heard his voice convey so much excitement. From that moment on, I spoke with Avi more than anyone else in Washington.

The next few weeks would be exhilarating, even if the center of negotiations moved from Jerusalem to Washington. David and Tammy Friedman had flown to the United States to see family, and I was again focused mainly on the U.S.-Israel relationship, which now included helping Israel get Covid vaccines when they became available and sharing therapeutics with the United States. I also spent a considerable amount of time working on technology sharing between Israel and the United States, to secure our technological superiority in the years to come. In other words, I was back to business more or less as usual while exciting progress was being made in the United States between Ambassador Al Otaiba, Ambassador Dermer, Jared Kushner, Avi Berkowitz, and David Friedman.

28

THE PHONE CALL

By August 2020, I was in and out of the Prime Minister's Office with great frequency, relaying messages from Jared, Avi, or David, or just making sure that there was a personal connection while David was in the States. I still got a thrill every time my phone rang with "Unknown" calling, which more likely than not was the Prime Minister's Office. Several times I drove or was driven more than two hours in heavy traffic from Raanana to Jerusalem only to be told that David had just called and spoken to the prime minister, or that Avi and Ron Dermer had called in together. I took it in stride, in the philosophy I had learned from David. Early in 2017, President Trump called him at three in the morning and he answered on the first ring. The president asked if it was the middle of the night in Israel, and David replied, "Mr. President, I work for you 24/7. Please call whenever you want." In that spirit, I usually picked up on the first ring whenever Jared, Avi, David, or the Prime Minister's Office called. I didn't hesitate to jump into the car to drive an hour for a five-minute meeting and then back again. I was willing to fly to Washington if a twenty-minute face-to-face meeting could accomplish more than countless emails and phone calls.

I was in a meeting with David Milstein and Israel's Innovation Authority on August 11, discussing the best way to fast-track breakthroughs in Covid-19 therapies made in Israel with the Innovation Authority's funding, when my phone rang. It was 3:30 p.m., and Friedman was calling. Normally I would pick up right away, but this time I didn't because I was in the middle of a meeting. He rang three more times, which was unusual for him, so I excused myself and went out to return the call.

"There has been a change in schedule," he told me. "The phone call with the UAE, Israel, and us is happening this week. Get to D.C. now." The crown prince of the United Arab Emirates, Sheikh Mohammed bin Zayed, would be participating in a call with Prime Minister Netanyahu and President Trump, and it would happen on August 13, just two days away.

I was in Tel Aviv without a passport, wallet, or plane ticket. I needed to get a PCR test for Covid and tackle some other logistical challenges. But when David told me to jump, my response was always "How high?"

I ran back into the meeting, apologized for having to step away, and committed to rescheduling in the near future. I called Sandy at the embassy to help me. Sandy was the manager of the front office, with dozens of years of experience. If something needed to get done, between her and Jonathan Shrier, the deputy chief of mission, it got done. Sandy immediately secured a car and driver and an expediter, and arranged for the medical office to be ready to do a PCR in the next thirty minutes. Then I called Estee and explained that I was needed in Washington immediately. She knew not to ask why, but instead, "How can I help?" I asked her to pack my bags and get my passport ready. At this point I realized that I still didn't have a plane ticket, so I called the embassy travel team, whom I got to know very well over my four years, and they managed to book a seat for me on a flight that evening. I went to the embassy for the PCR test, then home to pick up my bags and passport, and made it to my flight just before the boarding gate closed. Sliding into my seat, I reflected with amazement that just seven hours earlier I had been sitting in a meeting in Tel Aviv with no intention of flying anywhere that evening.

On August 12, I got to the White House by 9 a.m. and parked myself in Avi's office in the Eisenhower Executive Office Building, where I met some people who would become my best colleagues for the remainder of the administration. They were the National Security Council team that focused on the Gulf. I already knew many of them in passing, as I had tried to become friends with as many people as possible when I came to Washington, but sadly the Israel-focused teams in D.C. didn't interact a lot with the Gulf-focused teams. In Avi's office that day I met Major General Miguel Correa and Mark Vandroff for the first time. Also in the room were Rob Greenway, Ryan Arant, Scott Leith, and Eddie Vazquez. Under Jared Kushner's leadership, these people became the core of the team effectuating what would be called the Abraham Accords.

We went to work on making sure the phone call would go off without a hitch the next morning. What was still to be decided was when to make a public announcement. Even with three countries involved, fewer than forty people knew about the call beforehand. Any one of them could have leaked a self-serving story, as happens all the time in Washington and in Israel, but they all kept the plan tightly under wraps. This allowed the White House to shape the narrative from the beginning.

That night I couldn't sleep. Everything was buttoned up and ready to go, but either the prime minister of Israel or the crown prince of the UAE could call the whole thing off at a moment's notice. Having worked with various important leaders over the past three years, I knew it was not unheard of for leaders to change their minds at the last minute. I had no control over what would happen in the next twenty-four hours, but I was confident that the leaders of Israel and the UAE would know that the United States was with them 100 percent on wherever this journey would lead. Once again, it was the close relationships developed by Jared, David, Avi, and their teams that allowed an impossibly complicated phone call to go off without a hitch.

I was at the White House at 7:00 the next morning, though my entry permit was not good until 7:30. The entire team was in Avi's office by 8:15 to plan the rest of the day minute by minute. It was about 9:40 when we began to realize that what was about to happen was momentous enough to merit a name. Usually, a name for a government initiative of this kind would start with branding experts, then test-marketing, and finally a lengthy process for all the principal parties to give their approval. We had only twenty minutes. Various suggestions were made, and then Miguel Correa said, "The Abraham Accord. We are all children of Abraham. It is what unites us. That is what we should call this." There was immediate agreement among the team. With only twenty minutes until the call, we still needed President Trump, Israel, and the UAE on board with the name. As we walked over to the West Wing, Miguel called the UAE, Friedman called Israel, and Avi rushed to share the name with Jared and the president. Within two minutes we had consensus on the name. The smooth way this decision was made foreshadowed the fruitful cooperation that I would personally witness over the next 120 days.

As we were getting seated in the Oval Office and waiting for the phone call to begin, Jared asked, "Is this the Abraham Accord or the Abraham *Accords*?" Everyone seemed to know what he was thinking: it should be *Accords*, because more countries could and should participate. While the plural would put pressure on the

White House to get more participants, it would also signal to other countries that they could join if they wanted to.

At 10:00 a.m. promptly, President Trump led the call between Prime Minister Netanyahu and Sheikh Mohammed bin Zayed, which lasted about twenty-five minutes. In some respects it was like the conference calls you may have had with business associates or relatives, where awkward moments of silence are followed by two or three people talking at once. Many platitudes were spoken, but what I recall most vividly is the crown prince of the UAE saying that the year 2020 would be remembered for the pandemic that afflicted the whole world, but also for the moment when the people on this call chose to make a better future for their children and for the whole region.

At the conclusion of the call, the president pressed the hang-up button twice—you can never be too certain. We had no script for what would happen next, and at first everyone was quiet. Then Steven Mnuchin said, "Congratulations, Mr. President," and led everyone in a prolonged standing ovation. Many people in the room had tears in their eyes. Dan Scavino invited Avi to release the president's tweet and White House statement. Moments later, the White House press corps were ushered into the Oval Office and the prospects of peace were broadcast to the world.

The official White House statement about the phone call expressed excitement about the new prospects for the future of the Middle East. It explained that Israel had agreed to suspend the application of sovereignty in the West Bank (Judea and Samaria) as per the Peace to Prosperity Vision, and would instead channel its energies into developing this new relationship and preparing for others to follow soon. The statement made clear that this accord was not meant as a substitute for resolving the Israeli-Palestinian dispute, and affirmed the Peace to Prosperity Vision as a realistic roadmap for peace in the region. It concluded by celebrating the opportunity to bring some light to the future in the darkness of a pandemic.

The phone call sent shockwaves around the world. Pundits who focused on Middle East peace did not think the Trump administration would be able to accomplish anything that was not unilateral with his perceived weakness heading into the election. The same pundits took it as gospel truth that regional peace could not be achieved without Palestinian-Israeli peace. These are people who devote their time to watching the region closely, and they were taken completely by surprise. The average news consumer was no doubt even more surprised. No one was anticipating an announcement of this magnitude. To tell the truth, I believe that most people who worked on the steps leading up to the call didn't know how far the message of peace during these challenging days in August would resonate among the American people or across the Middle East and North Africa region. I think there was a feeling that this was going to be an important step toward a real change in the MENA region, but I don't think anyone felt it would be a hinge of history for the entire region. Being in the room for that historic phone call was one of the highlights of my life. I'll always be grateful to Friedman, Kushner, and Berkowitz for making sure I would be there for that moment.

29

ACCORDS, PLURAL

The following Monday, August 17, Jared had Avi, Miguel Correa, and me in his office to discuss the actions that we needed to take now to translate the phone call into practical results. The White House statement called for immediate actions by the UAE and Israel, and the United States was committed to facilitating these actions to fulfill the commitments stipulated in the agreement. The commitments included the development of diplomatic, trade, and security relationships, in addition to a joint task force to combat Covid-19. Jared asked Miguel to lead the implementation from the UAE and me to lead from Israel. Jared and Avi would be working with Ambassador Dermer and Ambassador Al Otaiba in D.C. to handle policy and politics.

Our guidelines for turning the Abraham Accord into the Accords were: Go fast, go big, and don't get caught up in politics. We had shocked the world hardly three days earlier, and those who wanted to detract from this development were still figuring out how to do it. Speed was going to be our friend. I spent the rest of that day in the White House coordinating with Correa, Berkowitz, Rob Greenway, and the National Security Council on the top ten achievable goals for the UAE and Israel, and with the list firmly in hand I caught the next flight out to Israel. The president also sent a loud and clear message that this was a priority, and Secretary Pompeo planned a trip to Israel and other countries in the region a week later.

Back in Israel, I had little time to reconnect with my family. Ambassador Friedman was still in the States, so my job was to explain to our embassy and the Israeli government what the next steps would be in this exciting chapter. My last five months at the embassy were particularly enjoyable. The Abraham Accords were just the pick-me-up the entire team needed after seven months of Covid-19 issues day in and day out. Our embassy became the busiest U.S. mission in the world bar none, and we promptly set the wheels in motion for Pompeo's upcoming visit. I was pleased that I would be accompanying him every step of his Israel trip since Friedman was out of the country, and this time it wouldn't come as a surprise.

What we needed to decide first was which country the secretary of state would visit after Israel. Within the peace team there was a debate about whether to concentrate our attention on developing the UAE-Israel relationship, or go straight to bringing other countries into the Accords. We knew that Bahrain and Oman were good prospects for joining in, and these possibilities were becoming public knowledge, but there was also a dark-horse candidate that no one would have guessed. Talks had been quietly going on with Sudan, which had recently ended the terror-supporting dictatorship of Omar al-Bashir and wanted to get out from under U.S. sanctions.

I told Secretary Pompeo that if he traveled to Sudan on this trip, we would make his plane the first direct flight there from Israel. He encouraged me to go for it and had me confer with his team. They were highly skeptical that it would be possible. In the past, the team in charge of the secretary's logistics had asked for direct flights from Israel to numerous countries that did not have relations with Israel, but without any luck. When cabinet members travel abroad, it makes sense to visit several other places in the same region. Countless hours and resources were wasted as long as the United States allowed other countries to tell our officials where they could and could not fly from to enter their airspace. I told Pompeo's team that I would take care of the flight permission.

As would happen so often over the next five months, I called Maoz. He said that a direct flight was possible and we would take care of it together. That evening we met at one of our usual places, and he pulled up phone number 3 to call the president of Sudan's chief of staff, General Sadiq. Our connection was not great, but I now realized that some of the crazy meetings that Maoz had me go to eighteen months earlier were beginning to pay dividends. I had met General Sadiq back then, and we would exchange greetings through Maoz from time to time. Once we got him on the phone, I told him that the secretary of state was planning on going to Sudan, as he knew, and that it would mean a great deal to me if the secretary could fly there directly from Israel without a technical stop. General Sadiq asked: Is this what's best for America? I said: Yes, it is. He replied, without hesitation, that I should consider it done. Now, that doesn't mean quite the same thing in Sudan as in some other countries, so I pushed a bit more: Could he assure me it was done? The general added the head of Sudanese aviation to the call and told him (as Maoz translated it) to do whatever the secretary of state's team wanted from him. And that was that. For decades this artificial boundary had stood between Israel and other countries—artificial for us, that is—and all it took to erase it was asking over a WhatsApp call.

Nonetheless, I was nervous about being responsible for the flight path of the secretary of state on the way from Israel to a country still technically at war with it. I remained uneasy until Morgan Ortagus sent me a message when the plane landed in Sudan on August 25: #Success #History! Finally I could exhale. From Sudan, Pompeo went on to Bahrain and the UAE, demonstrating that this was a priority of the Trump administration and letting other countries in the region know why we spoke about the Abraham Accords, plural.

30

EL AL TO ABU DHABI

M eanwhile, we knew that we needed to move rapidly to effect real changes, so we began planning to send a delegation to the UAE. Jared wanted an image of an El Al flight landing in the UAE, but the phone call between the prime minister and the crown prince had changed nothing legally. I told Jared and Avi that if they led a delegation from the White House to Israel, an Israeli delegation would join them in traveling to the UAE. Jared and Avi were thinking strategically, and they understood the value in a picture showing an El Al plane on the tarmac at the Abu Dhabi airport. This picture would accelerate the development and expansion of the Accords. He asked how soon we could make the flight happen logistically, and I said as soon as he had three days open in his schedule. He and Avi gave me a date five days away and said, "Make it happen." So we did.

In a short period of time, Israelis needed to procure a plane, appoint a head of delegation, get approval for travel during Covid-19, and so on. The UAE needed to decide what should be accomplished with this delegation. Those of us representing the United States also had to decide what our chief goals were. We wrote long to-do lists and began checking off items, and whenever we accomplished something we thought of ten others that needed to be done. The biggest challenge seemed to be whether the White House could secure permission for El Al to travel through Saudi airspace, which would cut the flying time from six and a half hours to three. It turned out not to be a challenge at all for Jared and Avi to get overflight permission over the Kingdom of Saudi Arabia.

For all three countries, nearly every decision involved a political calculus. Israel, with its fractious unity government, had difficulty deciding on personnel. The UAE contended with the risks of being the first Gulf country to take a major step toward peace in the region. The United States had a bandwidth issue as President Trump was heading toward a challenging election, dealing with Covid-19, and reaching an inflection point with the Islamic Republic of Iran.

The United States and Israel had an exceptionally close relationship during the Trump presidency, and the teams from each country had been working well in sync. The U.S. and UAE teams had also worked in sync. Now all of these groups needed to start working together for the first time, and it was like building the airplane while flying. There was no time to get acquainted or worry about formalities. We had only five days before the first flight of an Israeli plane over Saudi Arabia to the United Arab Emirates, with high-level Americans and Israelis aboard. Avi Berkowitz played the crucial role in coordinating the various teams, and he demonstrated his versatility as more countries were brought into the Accords. Avi was the problem solver as new issues kept popping up like whack-a-mole, while Rob Greenway from the NSC was the glue that kept the machinery in functional alignment.

The White House delegation turned out to be larger than anyone anticipated. Frankly, it was poor anticipation. Who would want to miss this historic flight? Leading the delegation were Jared Kushner, Robert O'Brien, Avi Berkowitz, and Adam Boehler, CEO of the Development Finance Corporation. There were NSC luminaries too numerous to list, but every one of them essential to accomplishing the mission. Because the delegation was so big, I had a lot to manage, being the pivot point for the U.S. Abraham Accords team concerning all Israeli decisions.

Upon arriving in Israel on August 30, the U.S. group had dinner with the prime minister. I knew that the requested menu on a Kushner visit would be hamburgers, and the informality made the working dinner much more enjoyable. When everyone is picking up hamburgers in their hands to bite in, perhaps leaving a little ketchup on the corner of their mouth, all pretention goes out of the room. Afterward, we visited the City of David. It was there, on behalf of David Friedman, that I presented a flag that flew over the U.S. Embassy in Jerusalem to Robert O'Brien and another one to Jared Kushner.

Jared's flag held special significance, having flown over the embassy on August 13, the day of the phone call that kicked off the Abraham Accords. In my brief presentation, I observed that the flag symbolizes so much to so many people. Around the world and at home, it stands for freedom and opportunity. It is probably the most admired symbol in the world, and rightly so. I felt it was important to bestow this flag on Jared at the site of the Pilgrimage Road, as I thought about the earliest Pilgrims who crossed an ocean seeking a new land, bringing the message, the values, and the direction of God himself with the aim of building a new Israel. The United States of America began with this guiding light and grew to become the greatest force for good in history, and if we hold on to that guiding light, this nation will remain so for our children and our children's children. But if we do not maintain those guiding principles, the United States may go the way of prior empires and lose its place in the world as a right and just superpower.

To me, this flag presentation was one of the more touching commemorations we had, especially as the proof was in the pudding. The very next day we were departing on the El Al flight that would put the actualization of the Abraham Accords into warp speed. In his response, Jared commented that when you stand for something unapologetically it brings clarity to your foreign policy, and when that happens, the rest of the world knows how to respond.

We were about to head for the hotel when Jared said we should stop at the Western Wall. So we had the Secret Service and the Israeli security details do a quick advance, and we went there at 10:30 p.m. We stayed only a short time, but it made an indelible impression on me that Jared thought it appropriate to go to the Western Wall and offer prayers for success and peace. I cannot emphasize enough the change that had transpired since my early days at the embassy, when I was told that I couldn't visit the City of David as a U.S. diplomat. Now I was visiting the City of David and the Western Wall with White House officials, the evening before a direct flight from Israel to the UAE, which would have been unimaginable two years earlier.

Early the next morning, August 31, the motorcade arrived at the private airplane terminal where the U.S. and Israeli delegations would board the El Al plane for the flight to Abu Dhabi. This was the first time that most of the U.S. delegation would meet the Israeli delegation, who were mostly directors general of ministries. I had worked with the vast majority of these directors general during the past few years, so I found myself serving as the unofficial host and facilitator for the two delegations. On the plane we found an enormous amount of swag courtesy of the Israeli Ministry of Foreign Affairs and our good friend Paul

Packer. Everyone was taking selfies with seat partners and with commemorative plane tickets, all caught up in the moment. Even the press were having a great time. The flight attendants were torn between taking selfies with the delegations and getting us to sit down and buckle our seatbelts. When the pilot announced that El Al flight 971 would be making the first-ever direct commercial flight to the UAE from Israel, the entire plane broke out in applause. I have been on numerous flights where there was applause upon landing, but this was the first where people applauded on takeoff. As we settled into our seats and the pilot announced the flight path over Saudi Arabia, the enthusiasm was even more electric. Menus from the flight were passed around to be signed. Every Israeli director general asked if I could arrange a selfie with Jared Kushner, who accommodated everyone with a smile and an encouraging word about the hard work that lay ahead for them.

Upon arrival in Abu Dhabi, I turned on my phone to find twenty-five missed calls from Estee, which was not a good sign. I learned that there had apparently been a fire in a fast-food restaurant at the Abu Dhabi airport, but it was reported on CNN as simply an airport fire in the UAE. Estee had assumed that we were under attack, and when I didn't respond, she panicked. Of course she was relieved when I called back, and she rather sheepishly told me that she had called David Friedman in New York, where it was four in the morning. I politely asked her what she thought he could do about a problem in Abu Dhabi. In response, she wished me luck on our historic visit.

We were greeted royally in Abu Dhabi, with a Mercedes for everyone. Helicopters were crisscrossing the motorcade route, and police were stationed at every intersection. I am not sure if this was for security or for pomp and circumstance, but it was what you would expect for a head-of-state visit, and it made us all feel like rock stars. Ambassador John Rakolta and his wife met us at the airport. They and their team played an important part in the success of the visit.

The most senior members of the U.S. delegation went with Maoz and Meir Ben-Shabbat, the head of the Israeli delegation, to meet the national security advisor of the UAE, Sheikh Tahnoon bin Zayed. I walked with the rest of the Israeli delegation to the St. Regis in downtown Abu Dhabi for two negotiating sessions and a get-acquainted dinner. As you might expect, the St. Regis exudes sophistication and wealth, while the traditional garb of the Emiratis adds a sense of deep heritage. The Israelis were very American in their attire, and much more aggressive in their posture.

As the only American there from the White House team, I gathered up the U.S. Embassy staff on hand to help facilitate negotiations on eight topics ranging from diplomatic relations to space travel and the environment, and we divided ourselves among eight rooms. We had let everyone know that simply showing up was an impressive diplomatic feat and there was no pressure to reach any specific agreements that evening. My job was to make sure that we achieved our most basic goal without anything going off the rails. Jared had asked me to find meaningful deliverables by seizing upon workable prospects that emerged in the discussions. The people participating in these negotiations were excited to be there, but like most government teams without political cover they were highly risk-averse. The sessions ended with positive feelings but little progress beyond simply getting everyone around the table.

Then we broke for dinner. The entire hotel had been made kosher friendly so that no visitor would feel out of place. This was an extraordinary accommodation, especially on short notice. I met with the rabbi doing the kosher supervision and asked how it could have been possible to make everything kosher so quickly. He assured me that all was proper. On order of the crown prince himself, all of the plates, cups, and cutlery of the hotel had been replaced that morning and would not be used with anything that was not kosher for the duration of our stay.

The room was filled with fifty Emirati men and women in traditional dress and fifty Israelis in Western business attire. We did not have the plated meals typical of a formal government affair. Instead, servers came around with at least a dozen different dishes, including kebabs, chicken, sea bass, and delicious vegetables. If you were paying attention to details, you would have noticed that some guests had a different color of napkin, and the servers knew to bring us only the kosher options. This extra care to make everyone feel included was much appreciated. I was also heartened to see that most Israelis were declining wine when it was offered—a reciprocal polite gesture in gratitude for the hospitality shown to them in a Muslim country.

The conversation at my table was riveting, and though the dinner was supposed to last for about two hours, more than four had already passed when Maoz came running in to look for me. "Aryeh, we had a great dinner with TBZ [Tahnoon bin Zayed], but we now have instructions to finalize investment and banking memos this evening. Is that even possible?" No sooner had I finished speaking with Maoz than Jared Kushner called and delivered the message in more direct terms: "Find the teams, and stay with them until this gets done." I had never negotiated an international trade agreement, but I told Jared and Maoz the same thing: "I know the Israelis would stay up all night to get it done, and I assume that if the message came from UAE leadership, the Emiratis would as well. Let's get the smallest team that we can get this done with, and let's get it done."

We assembled a team of four Israelis, four Emiratis, and myself, and we commandeered the stately conference room on the second floor of the St. Regis, the kind of room you can imagine filled with smoke and very important people. There was no smoke, but there was lots of coffee and Diet Coke to fuel us. Over the next five hours, we hammered out the framework for two memoranda of understanding to be signed the next morning.

When I rode with the Israeli delegation to the airport, our pockets were stuffed with business cards and our phones were filled with selfies we would never have expected to get. We then took off on El Al flight 972, the very first commercial flight from the UAE to Israel. This time I was the only American aboard, which meant that the Saudis were allowing overflight even for a delegation that was primarily Israeli.

As we landed in Israel, the pilot said he had one more announcement to make. He called up the lead flight attendant, who had served El Al for forty years and was retiring after this flight. The classically tough El Al flight attendant broke down in tears and said proudly in Hebrew, "I have flown Israel's national carrier for forty years, longer than anyone else who has worked for El Al, and never in my wildest imagination did I think I would lead an El Al crew on a plane to and from the UAE, flying over the Kingdom of Saudi Arabia. I have never been more proud to be an Israeli and represent El Al. Thank you." The entire plane once again broke into applause, along with tears and fist bumps.

31

BUILDING MOMENTUM

On the ground in Israel, we were jolted into reality again, having to do our daylong quarantine and mandatory PCR testing instead of a victory lap. Then it was back to work. We were now working on several fronts, trying to add more countries to the Abraham Accords while making sure that the UAE and Israel maintained their momentum.

While all of this was proceeding rapidly, economic normalization agreements with Serbia and Kosovo were being finalized. The negotiations were led by Ric Grenell, acting director of national intelligence and former ambassador to Germany. On September 4 came the announcement that Kosovo, a Muslim country in Europe, would fully normalize relations with Israel, and Serbia would move its embassy in Israel to Jerusalem. These milestones could not have been achieved without the momentum created by the Abraham Accords and the clear policy of the Trump administration that you cannot elevate your relationship with the United States in a vacuum. It matters how you treat our friends and allies, and Israel is a good litmus test of how you treat them.

Ric Grenell was a highly effective ambassador to Germany, helping to shape U.S. policy toward Germany specifically and

other parts of Europe as well. Like my boss, he had close connections to the White House and was a strong voice on behalf of
the administration's goals. One action that resonated with me
was his response to a statement by the German anti-Semitism
commissioner saying it was not safe for Jews to wear a kippa
in public in Germany. Ric tweeted: "The opposite is true. Wear
your kippa. Wear your friend's kippa. Borrow a kippa and wear
it for our Jewish neighbors. Educate people that we are a diverse
society." He then borrowed a kippa and wore it in public for an
entire day. An action like that is what we want from American
leadership but have too seldom seen. Ric, much like my boss
David, broke the mold of a traditional ambassador and they both
became much admired by members of the administration and
regular citizens around the world.

On the heels of the successful delegation to Abu Dhabi, the
White House would host a signing ceremony for the Abraham
Accords on the South Lawn, on September 15. It had been more
than twenty years since the last peace deal between Israel and
another country in the region. We knew that representatives
from the UAE and Israel would be at the ceremony, but we also
anticipated that at least one more country might choose to participate. This was not unfounded optimism, but was based upon
countless conversations involving Jared and Avi and the ambassadors of several relevant countries. Prime Minister Netanyahu
and his Mossad had been developing relationships with those
countries for a decade or longer. Maoz and his network of contacts throughout the region were also pushing for a breakthrough.
Not surprisingly, it was our friends and allies from Bahrain who
took the next step forward, agreeing to come to the White House
ceremony and sign the Accords themselves.

In a very short time, Jared and the White House team put
together an event that signified one of the great moments of

President Trump's time in office. In less than forty-five days, the president and his team facilitated the signing of major peace agreements between Israel and two Gulf countries, and there was a confident feeling that we were not done yet. The volume of phone calls I was receiving from more than ten countries that have not yet normalized with Israel as of this writing told me there was more to come. The greatest flurry of successful Middle East diplomacy occurred over a span of about seventy-five days.

After the signing ceremony, the embassy team returned to Israel on Netanyahu's plane. I remember being pretty annoyed that I was seated in economy after all my work on the Accords, while many people who knew basically nothing about them were in business. When I called Estee and complained about it, she reminded me, "You are flying on the prime minister of Israel's plane on the way back from a peace signing ceremony at the White House, in the middle of a worldwide health pandemic. Does it really matter how you fly?" She was correct, of course. I was back in Israel just in time for Rosh Hashana, and what better way to go into the Jewish New Year than seeing the Abraham Accords come into bloom!

Around this time, Jared recommended that Secretary Pompeo appoint me as the special envoy for the Abraham Accords. I began functioning in that capacity as early as September 20, even though I didn't get the official title of Special Envoy for Economic Normalization until December. Our instructions from the Oval Office were to keep pushing as fast as we could. The goal was to actualize the existing Accords as broadly as possible while keeping the door open for more countries to join if the opportunity arose. Jared made it clear that if the initial participating countries saw substantial dividends, other countries would join too. He was exactly correct. My tagline became: "Peace is not a Republican ideal, it is not a Democratic ideal, it is a core American value, and we will pursue real peace every chance we can." I helped coordinate the first El Al flight to Bahrain, the first Abraham Accords Business Summit in Abu Dhabi, the first direct flight to Israel on Etihad (the UAE's national carrier), the first Bahraini delegation to Israel, arriving on the first direct flight of Gulf Air (the Bahraini national carrier), the first direct El Al flight from Israel to Morocco, and the signing of more than a dozen memoranda of understanding.

32

SAKHIR PALACE

O ne of my primary tasks was to smooth the bumpiness on the road to normalization. That meant helping the two sides overcome decades of hostility and distrust. The negotiating teams for the Israelis and the Bahrainis were communicating, but the phone calls were leading to more confusion than clarity, and frustration was boiling over. I told both sides that moving the ball down the field would require sitting face to face, immediately. That was 9:00 p.m. on September 22.

Miguel Correa, the Middle East director on the National Security Council, was already on the ground in Bahrain leading the normalization effort there, and he was determined to match the Israel-UAE momentum. Major General might be his title—and a well-deserved one at that—but Correa fancies himself a cross between a professor and your cool uncle. Still, the two stars he earned in the U.S. Army add about six inches to his presence. No doubt the only person involved in these negotiations who could have taken Correa in a back-alley brawl was Sheikh Nasser bin Hamad Al Khalifa, the fourth son of King Hamad, and Bahrain's lead for the normalization process. Hollywood couldn't cast a more dashing Arab chief if auditions went on for a year: tall, dark, and handsome, with an infectious smile and loads of charisma.

Sheikh Nasser asked that the Israeli team arrive in Bahrain the next day by 10:00 a.m. Most of us had become accustomed to making last-minute adjustments to our schedules, as this was far from the first occasion that the timeline for normalization had been accelerated beyond reasonable expectations. There were myriad obstacles to making this happen in a flash: No visas. No flights. No overflight permission from Saudi Arabia. And no formal relations between Israel and Bahrain. Still, I told the Israelis to get a plane and gather a team of people who would not leak a bit of information. We couldn't afford a single misstep so early in the normalization process. I told the Israelis that if they could secure a plane, I would take care of the overflight permission. But how does a senior advisor to the most pro-Israel ambassador in American history "take care of" Saudi overflight? Simple: I called Avi Berkowitz.

Avi, now thirty-two, once had one of the hardest jobs in Washington. At the beginning of his White House career, his responsibilities were so wide-ranging and his contacts so extensive that he never knew whether a phone call would be a request for coffee or a very important message from a world leader to communicate to President Trump. Through all the ups and downs, Avi demonstrated tremendous loyalty to the White House, giving his whole self to the administration.

I explained the situation to Avi. He made two phone calls, and by midnight the Israelis had gotten a plane and I had a chief point of contact in Saudi Arabia. My contact and I were in communication until 6:00 a.m., figuring out all the minutiae of allowing an Israel-flagged carrier to fly over Saudi Arabia for the first time. It was just four hours before we needed to be on the ground in Bahrain.

I was exhausted, unshaven, and starving when I arrived at the ominously named Fatal terminal at Ben Gurion Airport. Nine Israelis would be traveling with me. Expecting to fly on a nondescript Gulfstream or some other small, private jet, I was horrified when we pulled up on the tarmac to a hulking Boeing 737 from the Israir fleet. One essential condition for a secret, nonofficial flight would be literally staying under the radar. This was critical for Israel, which did not have its usual security blanket expanded to Bahrain. It was also critical for Bahrain, which no doubt had been anticipating a higher-level first flight, like the one that carried a large White House delegation along with Israeli officials to the UAE. Maoz and I are great as a team, but we could not deliver the kind of peace dividend that would come to Bahrain a month later with an official direct flight led by Secretary Mnuchin and Israel's national security advisor, Meir Ben-Shabbat.

With all this weighing on my mind, I boarded the 737 to find the flight crew dressed in full hazmat suits. Not just gloves and masks, but the whole shebang: full-body onesies with face shields and goggles. Doctors treating Ebola patients have worn less protective gear!

The ten of us got settled quickly and the flight took off at 7:30 a.m. It was to take precisely two hours and eleven minutes, getting us to Manama soon enough that we could be at Sakhir Palace in western Bahrain by 10:15. I needed to get some sleep so I could be fully on my game when we arrived, and I quickly conked out.

I woke up at 8:15 and was alarmed to see the flight path screen showing that we were still over Israel. We should have been leaving Jordanian airspace for Saudi airspace around that time. I sprinted to the cockpit and asked our pilot what the heck was going on. Had the Saudis rescinded overflight privileges at the last minute? I was ready to call Avi in Washington, where it was 2:15 a.m.

It turned out that no one had informed Jordan about the flight, and because this was during the pandemic, the head of Jordanian air traffic control was on an alternative schedule and hadn't yet arrived at work. After all-night negotiations involving the White House, the Israeli Prime Minister's Office, and the chief of Saudi aviation, it was the Jordanians, with whom Israel has enjoyed peaceful relations for a quarter century, who were the obstacle, if unwittingly.

Once we finally received clearance to cross Jordan, it was a smooth ride over Saudi Arabia. We knew it was inevitable that "plane watchers," the people who track and speculate about the intentions of every flight from Israel, would soon report our transit. What was most crucial was whether anyone on the team would reveal who was on the plane and what we were doing. Discretion was key to our mission.

Upon arrival in Bahrain, we were escorted to the palace, where the Israeli negotiating team sat down with the Bahraini team for their first serious negotiations. The Bahraini hospitality was amazing, and I was pleased to meet up again with leaders who had attended the Peace to Prosperity Workshop fifteen months earlier. I was quite comfortable with both our Israeli and Bahraini allies, and I felt even better knowing that Miguel Correa and John Rader, another invaluable member of Kushner's team, were going to be with me during the negotiations. What caught me by surprise was that we were joined by an Israeli diplomat who had been undercover in Bahrain (known only to the Bahrainis and to one Israeli in the room).

This meeting would demonstrate the need for the United States to play a role in advancing the Accords, since the Bahrainis and Israelis approached the negotiations in very different ways. The Bahrainis were much like anyone with an MBA from the top schools in the world, bringing a methodical approach to the entire process of normalization. They were organized, clearly operating under tight controls on who could do what, and when. The Israelis were the opposite of methodical. Instead, they were innovative, and disruptive in a good way. We were operating in unusual circumstances, what with Covid-19, new relationships in the Middle East, and a backdrop of security concerns, mostly emanating from Iran but also from other nefarious actors. These circumstances played to the Israelis' strengths, particularly their ability to adapt. However, we were up against a clock. Who knew how much more time the Trump administration would have, or how long this ride toward peace would last without a major hiccup or worse? This factor played to the strength of the Bahrainis, their methodical discipline.

The negotiations lasted a whole day, the first three-quarters of which were consumed in talking at each other. But the last quarter brought the major breakthrough, when each side recognized the strengths the other side was bringing to the table and saw the great potential in combining them. I have full confidence in the capabilities of both sides, but it was Correa, Rader, and I who kept everyone's eyes on the prize so the negotiations could proceed fruitfully.

A highlight of the visit was our meal as guests of Sheikh Nasser. I cannot speak for everyone, but I was not accustomed to dining in the palace of a king as the guest of his son. We were quickly put at ease by the hospitality of Sheikh Nasser and his very senior team, Sheikh Salman bin Khalifa Al Khalifa and Sheikh Abdulla bin Ahmed bin Abdulla Al Khalifa, whom I consider a dear friend and colleague. Picture this: an American two-star general, an advisor from the U.S. National Security Council, and the senior advisor from the U.S. Embassy in Jerusalem dined with ten Israelis and ten Bahrainis in King Hamad's palace as guests of Sheikh Nasser, and it felt surprisingly normal.

There was one moment of awkwardness, however. We all sat around a lavish, beautifully decorated table, fit for a king, and waited for Sheikh Nasser to take the first bite. After he did so, many people at the table turned in my direction to see what I would do. The food looked delicious, I must say, but I knew that it wasn't kosher because the visit had been planned only at the last minute. I picked up my fork, then put it down. I wasn't going to play the game of just moving food around on the plate. Sheikh Nasser asked Sheikh Abdulla why I wasn't eating, and Sheikh Abdulla whispered to him that the food wasn't kosher. Sheikh Nasser looked at the Israelis, most of whom were eating, and then back at me, and then at Sheikh Abdulla, who then looked at me too. All I could do was shrug my shoulders. It was ironic that the American diplomat had more of an issue with non-kosher food than many of the Israelis. The awkwardness quickly dissipated, and I enjoyed hearing stories about the history of Bahrain while the others savored the meal. Then the conversation moved back to the Abraham Accords, and we started mapping out the next one hundred days.

After dinner, we took a picture together at the palace exit, all feeling that we had been part of something historic and important. As Sheikh Abdulla escorted me to a chauffeured Mercedes-Maybach—who said that negotiating in the Gulf didn't have perks?—he put his hand on my shoulder and promised that I would have kosher food whenever I visited Bahrain in the future, as he and Sheikh Nasser were committed to making me feel at home. This comment floored me. It wasn't part of the Abraham Accords. It didn't have anything to do with security or economics. In fact, it didn't appear that any of the Israelis cared whether the food was kosher or not. Yet Sheikh Abdulla knew that for real peace to happen, everyone would need to feel comfortable, and that included making sure that people committed to eating kosher would have kosher food. This was a sincere move, demonstrating that the fabric of peace would consist of genuine goodwill.

33

BUSINESS SUMMIT

B ecause of Covid-19 travel restrictions, the markets between Israel and the UAE and Bahrain could not develop in a normal way. The result was more opportunity for fraud and corruption, which would be the worst possible result of the Abraham Accords, leading to distrust and putting the momentum behind the eight ball. So we decided to host a business summit where we could connect the top business leaders and entities from Israel and the UAE. We planned to hold the event in Abu Dhabi and worked around the clock to make it a success. Secretary Mnuchin agreed to come as an anchor host from the White House, on his first international trip during Covid. We leveraged his trip to the region to launch the first direct flight from Israel to Bahrain, on October 18.

We spent twenty-four hours in Bahrain helping to facilitate negotiations between the Bahrainis and the Israelis, much as we had done with the UAE four weeks earlier. Then we flew on Mnuchin's plane to Abu Dhabi to run the first Abraham Accords Business Summit on October 19. It was held at the Emirates Palace Hotel, a facility that makes even the largest Las Vegas hotels look like roadside motels.

The summit was hugely successful. We had twenty-five of the top business leaders from both countries connecting, beginning to understand each other's culture, and agreeing to serve as a network for each other. Collectively they would vet and recommend responsible business partners. In the evening, Mnuchin delivered a message of peace and prosperity on behalf of the United States. Titans of industry in the audience were moved to tears, knowing that they were helping to propel the region toward a safer, stronger, and more prosperous future for their children.

Later that evening, a group from the peace team were in Avi Berkowitz's hotel room at the Emirates Palace negotiating on the phone with the Sudanese. The traveling physician was doing Covid-19 tests and I asked to go first, since I was to meet with Adam Boehler that evening. The physician agreed, and thirty minutes later on the dot I heard a stern order: "Lightstone, leave the room now!" When I saw the doctor's face, I instantly knew he wasn't kidding. My Covid test had come back positive.

All at once I was flooded with emotions. That day I had met with three senior Emirati ministers, and then had dined with fifty of the most influential businesspeople from the United States, Israel, and the UAE, as well as our secretary of the treasury and ambassador to the UAE. I knew that Covid wasn't my fault, but I couldn't begin to comprehend the disaster I might have been responsible for as a practical matter. The physician told me to isolate, but added that the test system we were using had a 2 percent false positive rate. He had never seen a false positive, but maybe I was the first. I took a second test and prayed like I had not prayed in a long time, though not for myself particularly. I felt fine and was in great shape then, and I realized that quarantining at the Emirates Palace for two weeks was probably not the worst thing in the world. Instead I prayed for the White House team led by Avi and Miguel Correa so we could go close Sudan. I prayed for

Mnuchin, who took an enormous personal risk by being away from D.C. within two weeks of the election. I prayed for the Emiratis I had spent the day with and hoped their feelings about the Abraham Accords wouldn't be diminished if they wound up in quarantine because they came to the business summit.

After thirty-one of the longest minutes of 2020, the physician knocked on my door. "Lightstone, you are good to go," he said. "The first test was a false positive, this one is negative, but let's do one more to be sure." I let out a sigh of relief and would have hugged him if it weren't inappropriate. Then I called Adam Boehler and told him I would be ready to meet in half an hour, after the third Covid test.

Adam sketched out his vision for what would be called the Abraham Fund, a project of the Development Finance Corporation of America. When Congress established the DFC, it was to provide an economic tool for the U.S. government to use in promoting the national interest around the world. Adam was the CEO, and with his business acumen and leadership the DFC became one of the most effective instruments the U.S. government had in its soft diplomacy toolkit. Adam wanted to leverage the momentum of the Abraham Accords, and the best way to do that was by setting up a fund with Israel, the UAE, and Bahrain, to do joint deals. The fund would be based in Jerusalem, and it could provide a professional and organized methodology for these countries to start working together. It could also provide the capital to push deals over the finish line and give assurance to wary individuals that their governments are fully on board with normalization. Adam and I spoke into the wee hours to develop a constructive game plan for the Abraham Fund. We only needed someone to run it.

Throughout the day, I had been exchanging WhatsApp messages with someone my dear acquaintance Eli insisted I meet.

Eli is probably the most unassuming successful person I know. He is also a rarity as a Modern Orthodox Jew from New York who is perhaps most comfortable speaking Arabic and lounging at the home of a sheikh. This is what had made him a mainstay of the Persian Gulf for many years already. Eli tries to connect me with one of his friends wherever I travel, and on this trip he pleaded with me to spend just twenty minutes with his friend Hamad. So Hamad and I settled on meeting for coffee at seven the next morning.

I was running late in the morning, as usual, and didn't allow sufficient time to navigate the enormous hotel. While speed-walking toward the café, I chatted with a few friends from the White House and did a humblebrag that I was meeting with a local Emirati. It was always fun to see people's reactions when they learned that the Israel-based, Orthodox Jewish U.S. diplomat had more locals coming to meet him than the people stationed in the region.

But there's a risk in getting too far out over your skis. I got to the café at 7:20 and didn't succeed in connecting with Hamad. I sent him another message. No response. I called him. Still no response. I had been stood up! I would have to admit to my friends from the White House that I actually didn't have friends or contacts in Abu Dhabi.

Twenty minutes later, I received a message from Hamad.

"Thanks for breakfast. It was great meeting you."

I had heard of Arab hospitality, but this was ridiculous. We hadn't even met, and he was thanking me for breakfast! I called Hamad again, and this time he answered.

"Where are you this very moment?" I asked.

"I just left having breakfast with you," he replied. "What do you mean?"

"Stand still. I'm coming to find you."

I ran out to the lobby and found Hamad. He looked me up and down, and I looked him up and down, and he asked, "Are you Aryeh?"

"I am."

Puzzlement swept across his face. "Well, who did I have breakfast with?"

"I'm not sure! You were supposed to have breakfast with me."

"Eli told me to look for the most important person in the room and that would be you," he said, shrugging his shoulders.

Ah, I thought I saw the problem. I pulled out my phone and showed Hamad a picture of Secretary Mnuchin, and anxiously asked, "Is this the guy?"

"Yes, I had breakfast with him!"

We both roared with laughter.

A little later I was boarding an Etihad plane along with Mnuchin, Berkowitz, Boehler, the White House peace team, and four senior Emirati ministers for the first official UAE delegation to Israel. I didn't know what to expect. Would the Emiratis have the same excitement about going to Israel as the Israelis had in going to the UAE? The answer was decisively yes. The ministers and their teams were eager to push forward the vision of their leadership to create a safer, stronger, more prosperous Middle East.

When the plane landed, we were greeted by Ambassador Friedman and Prime Minister Netanyahu. There were a few speeches before the trilateral meetings were to begin. The last speech was by Adam Boehler, who spoke about the launch of the $3 billion Abraham Fund, and said it would be run by Aryeh Lightstone. I had hoped he would consider me for the position, but I didn't expect to be given the job on live international TV. So my ego was restored.

34

SUDAN IN TRANSITION

I had already traveled with a very small group of Americans and Israelis to Sudan to hammer out a peace treaty. Sudan had special meaning since its capital city, Khartoum, was where the Arab League met after the Six-Day War in 1967 and declared, "No peace with Israel, no recognition of Israel, and no negotiations with Israel." Sudan was still technically in a state of belligerence with Israel, unlike the UAE, Bahrain, Morocco, or Kosovo.

Sudan did not actually set out to make peace with Israel. Its only motivation for doing so was to join the community of nations after decades of decay, dictatorship, and disarray. Sudan under the rule of Omar al-Bashir was well known for harboring terrorists. The United States imposed sanctions, with the result that a wealthy country saw its resources depleted to nearly nothing and was closed off from the free world. After al-Bashir was overthrown in 2019, an interim government was cobbled together, and it tried to meet the requirements that the United States laid out for rejoining the community of nations and being rid of sanctions. One of those requirements was to normalize relations with Israel.

Many pundits thought it was too high a bar for Sudan's transitional government to meet. Why mix Israel in with a struggling country in the middle of Africa? The answer is simple: We either do or do not stand with our friends. If we stand consistently with Israel, then normalizing with Israel must be a condition for joining the community of nations.

On my second secret flight to Sudan, on November 23, it was clear that we were in make-or-break territory. The clock was ticking on the president's ability to expend more bandwidth on countries that were on the brink of joining the Abraham Accords but not there yet.

The flight from Israel carried three U.S. government officials, all former Special Forces, and three Israelis, all from their country's Special Forces, and me, a rabbinic school graduate. As we were landing at Khartoum, the security team began strapping up like they were headed into a war zone. It was not a comforting sight. We were all given global satellite phones with emergency numbers. I told the security people that everyone else on the plane had substantial military experience, so their job was to keep me safe. Maoz laughed and said not to worry, he would look after me, which I found reassuring. Maoz was a VIP, but he had the look and confidence of someone who could take care of things if they went bad in a hurry. I decided that I would always stay within five feet of either Correa or Maoz as long as we were in Sudan.

At the Khartoum airport, the only other plane on the tarmac that looked like it could actually fly was from Air Syria. I was reassured to see a convoy of white SUVs ready to transport us in a motorcade. After deplaning, I saw my friend General Sadiq and gave him a big hug. He directed me to a car and I got in. I waited for the security to join me, but they were directed to another car, and the motorcade took off. I figured I was fine with my satellite phone. It wouldn't turn on, though. Apparently the batteries were not charged. Still, I was in a motorcade of armored cars and we were all together, so I would be fine. Then my car and the two behind it got cut off in traffic and had to make a detour to catch up.

Going through what looked like a suburban area, we came upon a makeshift roadblock manned by two individuals who couldn't have been older than seventeen. They had shopping carts full of RPGs at each end of their blockade, which got our attention. My driver pulled up to one of them and rolled down his window. This was the last straw for me, since the windows of armored cars cannot be rolled down. All of my security assumptions went out that window. The one option we had left was speed. Using the only word we had in common, I told the driver: *Go*. And he went—speeding around the roadblock and the teenagers with their RPGs, and racing through the neighborhood. Somehow we caught up with the motorcade just as it pulled into the presidential compound.

Then we got down to the business of negotiating. I actually became quite fond of the Sudanese leadership. They were far from perfect, but they had enormous obstacles to surmount in the effort to make Sudan into a modern country with rights for most if not all of its 38 million people. They appeared willing to take the courageous steps necessary to move forward. But in spending time with them as they deliberated over policy decisions, I also realized why it is so easy for countries to slip into dictatorship. Simply put, a dictatorship is easier to manage. The transitional government of Sudan was struggling to feed the nation's people, and now trying to reach a consensus on normalizing relations with a country that it is still technically at war with. Such decisions are difficult for a committee, especially one without long experience of working together, but our negotiating team was impressed by how the Sudanese handled this challenge.

After hours of negotiating, the Sudanese agreed to everything we were offering in financial help and assistance in reentering the community of nations, in exchange for normalizing with Israel. But they thought we had not offered enough, and they asked for a bigger commitment to help them achieve stability. They also said they could not have a full peace agreement with Israel but were willing to sign a nonbelligerence agreement, meaning they would no longer threaten Israel militarily. Our team huddled and agreed that I would be the closing negotiator. This what I told the Sudanese:

> Every American is rooting for your success. We want to see a strong and proud and safe Sudan. It is good for you, good for your people, and good for us. However, there is a miscalculation of leverage here. We are the United States of America, and we have relations with nearly every country on earth, some productive and some less productive. We hope that all of these relationships grow and evolve and help us become more secure and prosperous. Out of all the countries in the world, the one that gives us the most reciprocity in our relationship is the State of Israel. They get an enormous amount of our attention because they contribute significantly to our growth, prosperity, and security. I landed at your airport, and it is important for you to know that two of my neighbors in Israel are F-35 pilots. Your offer of no longer threatening them militarily is kind, but unnecessary. Israel is a first-world military power, and you are trying to figure out how to feed your people breakfast tomorrow. We are not here to take baby steps. We are here to discuss a full peace opportunity. If a relationship with Israel is successful for us, it will be successful for you. I don't understand your internal politics, so you have to make the decision that is best for your country, but please understand that if we choose between Israel and Sudan, we will choose Israel every

time. Our plane must depart in ninety minutes, so we can discuss this for eighty minutes but then we will leave the compound. And unfortunately, we are unlikely to come back again. It is your choice, and we wish you well in your decision-making process.

The Sudanese negotiating team came back within ten minutes and accepted the original framework we offered. The average American may not have noticed the peace agreement between Israel and Sudan on October 23, but countries throughout Africa and the Middle East did.

35

OLIVE TREES

J ared and Avi came to Israel on December 22 to lead the first
El Al flight to Rabat, Morocco, the next day, leading up to
the signing of another peace agreement. First, the State of Israel
honored Jared with the planting of eighteen olive trees in a garden
reserved for heads of state, called the Grove of Nations. This was
a remarkable sign of how Israel viewed Jared's contribution to the
U.S.-Israel relationship. After the beautiful ceremony came the
somewhat awkward sight of world leaders in suits and facemasks
shoveling dirt to plant trees beneath anti-sniper tents. There were
no theater seats for the press and visiting dignitaries. When Jared
was thanking the prime minister, a reporter leaned on me to get
a better shot. My dress shoes slid on the wet dirt, and I stopped
myself from falling down only by leaning on Adam Boehler,
who managed to catch me and stop both of us from tumbling to
the ground. His shoes did get dirty in the process, and I felt bad
about it as they were much nicer than mine.

Afterward we went by motorcade to the U.S. Embassy, where
Ambassador Friedman officially inaugurated the Kushner Court-
yard. The courtyard is the great melting pot of the embassy.
Everyone from embassy workers to visitors to visa applicants will

wait or mingle there, and if you want a delicious cup of coffee, that is your only place to go. On any given day between 8 a.m. and 4 p.m. you will see every type of Israeli who wants a visa to the United States—Jewish, Christian, Muslim, Bahai, religious and nonreligious, men and women, children and elderly. There are also U.S. citizens of just as many different backgrounds who come for assistance. It is quite possible that the U.S. Embassy courtyard and the Ben Gurion Airport check-in lines draw the widest human spectrum seen in all of Israel. There are the normal frustrations with bureaucracy, red tape, language difficulties, and long lines, but everyone gets along remarkably well. It is a little like how I imagine a more perfect society would be. We decided to dedicate this courtyard in Jared's honor.

The dedication plaque is about 100 meters from where Jared gave one of the keynote speeches at the opening of the embassy on May 14, 2018. He said that the recognition of Jerusalem as the capital of Israel and the rapid opening of the U.S. Embassy there would bring peace in the region closer. This line was used in the media along with a split screen juxtaposing video from the embassy opening with scenes of terrorists in Gaza rushing the border into Israel. It was therefore fitting to honor Jared in this specific location for being vindicated.

The following day, the first El Al flight to Rabat culminated in renewed diplomatic relations between the Kingdom of Morocco and the State of Israel. This was the fifth agreement signed between Israel and an Arab/Muslim country in less than a hundred days. Israel's normalized ties with the United Arab Emirates, the Kingdom of Bahrain, Serbia and Kosovo, Sudan, and Morocco are not a cold peace as we have seen between Israel and Egypt or Jordan. They are a warm peace, the type of peace that allies have and that friends aspire to have.

36

KEYS TO SUCCESS

I t was widely believed that the materialization of the Abraham
Accords was basically just luck, but that could not be further
from the truth. There were particular reasons for this foreign policy success. One key was the absence of a public process, because
the only good that comes from such processes in a volatile region
like the Middle East is job security for the people involved. Previous attempts at Middle East peace involved a myriad of public
confidence-inducing measures, and then pundits from across the
political spectrum and around the world would dissect every word
and action. As a consequence, words and actions became more
carefully scripted and rehearsed, with an eye to what the next
media take might be. Analysis then came pouring forth with all
the brilliance of the neighborhood fantasy football fanatic, while
peace remained ever elusive. So the Abraham Accords team took
a very different approach. There would be no public negotiations
and no strategic leaks through the press. The Accords would be
announced only when they were completed.

While the media speculated, fished, and occasionally made
stuff up, there were never any consequential leaks, let alone any
that derailed plans. Everyone involved in the peace plan had a

high-level security clearance, which meant that discretion was mandatory. What's more, the people involved in the Abraham Accords were all pleased to keep the necessary discretion rather than backstab colleagues, hurt allies, and damage the prospects for peace by selective leaks to certain media outlets. I believe this was crucial to success.

Another key was relying upon leaders of countries involved to be—wait for it—leaders. Instead of treating them as whipping boys or obstacles to progress, the White House empowered them, giving them broad leeway and public encouragement. They know their own countries and the needs of their people better than an assistant secretary of state who studied international affairs at an Ivy League school. The White House gave those leaders as much space as possible to negotiate on their own countries' behalf. That is a reason why each principal and senior staff member who participated kept the necessary discretion and secrecy.

Finally, the Abraham Accords came about because the United States under President Trump had a clear Middle East policy that let the world know who our friends and foes are, and the metrics for moving from one status to another. It was not a romantic Middle East policy, but a practical one. When there was a question of what we should do, the first consideration was not what the rest of the world would think, but what was in the best interest of the United States.

Experienced foreign policy experts, including career diplomats, can often lose sight of the national interest because they spend so much time abroad. The foreign service itself recognizes the risk of diplomats going native if they remain in one country too long, which doesn't mean becoming a spy or a double agent, but simply starting to advocate for the country they are posted to more than promoting the interests of the United States. This is why foreign service officers are assigned for tours of up to four years in one posting and rarely longer. Yet as we saw earlier, diplomats tend to socialize with other people in the diplomatic world and share a common outlook. There's a similar issue with people who spend many years in foreign policy think tanks. They can become so immersed in their think-tank universe that they are blinkered to the practical results of their policy prescriptions.

President Trump and his team of nonprofessional and inexperienced diplomats did not succeed in spite of their lack of experience; they succeeded because of their lack of experience. They were able to approach the challenges of the Middle East as businesspeople on behalf of the American public. Where are our interests, what motivates us, and what are our challenges? Once we address those questions, we have the ability to chart a course that works for us.

What followed was rather remarkable. Other nations may have been annoyed that we were suddenly pursuing a strong America-oriented foreign policy, but they could not argue with it, because it made sense. From the Jerusalem recognition through the release of the Peace to Prosperity Vision, our foreign policy was bold and decidedly America First. We could not expect other countries to be more pro-American than we are.

President Trump found the Middle East with an ISIS caliphate, Iran on a glidepath toward nuclear capability, the Muslim Brotherhood legitimized, Israel isolated, and the Palestinian leadership unaccountable to the United States or to their own people. He left the Middle East in a much different state. The ISIS caliphate was destroyed. Iran was brought to its knees. The Muslim Brotherhood were challenged to divorce radical Islamic ideology from their philosophy or not be considered a legitimate political influence. The Palestinian leadership were challenged to become accountable, and the Palestinian people were shown a vision of what the future could be. Israel became the undisputed regional superpower, and the Abraham Accords strengthened our other core allies in the region—the United Arab Emirates, Bahrain, and Morocco. In addition, Sudan and Kosovo viewed joining the Accords as a way to elevate their own status in the world.

Because the Middle East was trending in such a positive direction, I continued working in my embassy position as long as possible. My job was essentially to see that Israel was following through on its commitments to the other Abraham Accords countries. While the UAE, Bahrain, Morocco, Kosovo, and Sudan were each adjusting to just one new relationship, Israel had begun new relationships with five different countries in the span of 123 days. The Israeli government did everything in its power to develop these relationships at a time when every country was grappling with Covid-19 and international travel had nearly ceased.

Some of my colleagues expressed frustration on behalf of leaders in other Accords countries who complained that Israel was not very organized in its approach to normalization. This was a polite way of saying that Israeli politics were interfering with the process, which was indeed true. In a parliamentary democracy, the prime minister is surrounded by other ministers with substantial portfolios, many from a different political party, and in the cycle of constant elections it was rarely clear if these ministers were wearing their policy hats or their political hats. There was often frustration among the Israeli leadership, and occasionally some yelling. I spent an inordinate amount of my time working to make sure that the Israeli government communicated consistently and effectively to its Accords partners, regardless of the political leanings of any particular minister, ministry, or agency.

Meanwhile, each of the other Accords countries had its own specific lines of effort and chain of command. The ministry of economic affairs in the UAE, Bahrain, or Morocco would never call its counterpart in Israel, or anyone else in the Israeli government, without clearance by the team in charge of the Abraham Accords in that country, usually the foreign ministry. But ministers in Israel frequently reached out to their counterparts or other leaders in the UAE, Bahrain, or Morocco, to launch an initiative of their own. Sometimes it was a good thing, but sometimes it went at cross-purposes with the roadmap that the two countries had already agreed upon. Practically every other day I received a phone call from the White House team asking me to "control the Israelis." To which I replied, "If you think that is possible, you have ignored the past seventy-two years of Israeli history," and then added, "Don't forget which country in the equation is a democracy." Israel is a democracy, and democracy is messy. Political competition and contention will affect policy more than in other forms of government. The United States should understand and even celebrate this aspect of governance in another democratic country, no matter how maddeningly frustrating it can be.

I concluded my last Abraham Accords phone call at 5:45 p.m. on January 20, 2021. My letter of resignation would take effect at 7:00 p.m. Many people in the administration resigned when President Trump lost the election. Many others coasted until the end of the term. Some had professional bucket lists of items to cross off before leaving government, possibly forever. Not the Abraham Accords team. We kept working to the very last hour, repeating the mantra: "Peace is not a Republican ideal or a Democratic ideal, it is an American value."

37

STALLED MOMENTUM

Like Israel, the United States is a democracy, though a presidential rather than a parliamentary one, and our foreign policy changes with a new administration. As Americans, we are all free to express our opinions on what each administration is doing and what policies are best. I hope this book makes the case for the ideas and policies that I witnessed in real time to bring positive outcomes in the Middle East.

The Palestinians and the Iranians spent all of 2020 rooting for Joe Biden to be the next president, knowing that U.S. foreign policy would likely revert to pre-2017 policy. Here in the United States, the hope was that the Biden presidency would "bring the adults back into the room" and restore calm predictability. Some people thought President Biden would govern as a centrist, taking some of Trump's policies that were working well and making them his own. Unfortunately, the administration did not start out looking for broad bipartisan support. Whether it was the rush to prioritize reopening a consulate for the Palestinians in Jerusalem, seeking to reenter a nuclear deal with Iran, or choosing not to work with Mohammed bin Salman, the crown prince of Saudi Arabia, the Biden administration seemed to be pushing partisan buttons unnecessarily.

Some of the administration's first moves slowed the momentum of the Abraham Accords and diminished the possibility for expanding them further across the region. The Trump peace team had aimed to go big and go fast after the August 13 phone call because momentum was crucial to the growth of the Abraham Accords in a short period of time, especially with the global challenge of Covid-19. It was important to move quickly to demonstrate that benefits would follow from joining the Accords. Every country that had done so assumed some level of risk in exchange for the rewards baked into the agreements, such as more scientific and cultural exchange and increased tourism. These were all taken into account by participating countries when they entered the Accords. But where is the benefit to show other countries that they are missing out by not joining? Where is the peace dividend? This dividend was paid by the Trump administration in spades. In the precious time of its waning days, it gave attention to every country in the Accords and to most that were clearly thinking of joining.

On the other hand, President Biden did not recognize these countries in his address to a joint session of Congress in April 2021. He did not call their leaders to congratulate them. For months, he did not have his State Department reach out and see how best to continue the momentum. The Biden administration instructed embassies around the world to stop using the term Abraham Accords, and embassy staff who had been critical in the implementation and growth of the Accords were told that they were no longer essential to U.S. policy.

When Ned Price, the spokesperson for the State Department, refused to mention the Abraham Accords by name in response to a reporter's question, it appeared that politics were driving the foreign policy agenda of the United States. While the glib back-and-forth between Price and Matt Lee of the AP was entertaining to watch, it was heard loud and clear in Iran and the Palestinian territories. The thinking was: There is a new administration in town, we survived the past four years, and we look forward to thriving over the next four, perhaps more.

If peace with no strings attached cannot win bipartisan support from one administration to another—especially peace with Israel, the supposed bipartisan jewel of U.S. foreign policy—then what will? It is true that the Abraham Accords have received some measure of bipartisan support, such as the launching of the bicameral Abraham Accords Caucus in Congress, more than ten months after the phone call that set things in motion. I applaud this step, but it is difficult to imagine Middle East peace treaties occurring so rapidly under any other administration yet greeted so tepidly by the opposition party.

It is a disappointing fact that politics have become more personal and divisive over the past several years. In some places, whom you voted for defines who you are. People stopped speaking to my mother because I worked for President Trump. My career State Department colleagues who worked closely with me and other team members on the Abraham Accords and before that were demoted for it. I have chosen not to mention the names of many here because it would be damaging to their careers. Why that should be so in the United States in 2021 is incomprehensible to me.

I also believe that if it had been any other administration, not only would the president and the peace team have received a Nobel Peace Prize, but more importantly the leaders of the Abraham Accords countries would have become internationally acclaimed Nobel laureates. I think that it was only because they signed the Accords under President Trump's stewardship that they were denied the international acclaim and admiration that they so richly deserve.

I have been pleased to see that the Biden administration seems to be coming around in support of the Abraham Accords. A cynic might ascribe this change to the fact that the one-year anniversary of the Accords followed on the heels of the Afghanistan debacle. Yet since then, the administration has said more of the right things and taken some active steps forward, such as hosting a trilateral meeting in Washington with the foreign ministers of Israel and the UAE, and leading a virtual meeting with the foreign ministers of Morocco and Israel on the one-year anniversary of the Morocco normalization. I credit the administration for this change in stance, and I am optimistic about what might be ahead. Yet during the nine months in which the U.S. position on the Abraham Accords was vague, to say the least, other leaders made decisions and the Accords evolved to a great degree on their own.

It is decidedly in the interest of the United States to encourage other countries to join the Abraham Accords. More peaceful relations between countries in the region means less reason for U.S. troops to be stationed there. The American people, both Republican and Democrat, do not seem to favor keeping large numbers of U.S. troops permanently stationed in the Middle East and in harm's way. As the scope of the Accords expands, the area of potential friction in the Middle East shrinks. The more the Accords members work together across all fields and industries, including defense, the more our mere presence in combination with their fighting forces will serve as a deterrent to troublemakers in the Middle East. Our current geostrategic challenges lie primarily elsewhere in the world, and we need to be able to place our military assets strategically in those locations well in advance of a potential conflict, mostly to ensure that there will not be a conflict.

Finally, I think it pays to revisit our approach to our interests in the Middle East and how best to encourage trends that align with our values. For the past ten years, the largest survey of the Arab world's young people has found the UAE to be the country that the largest numbers would want to live in or have their home country emulate. Economically, culturally, and scientifically, the UAE has set itself apart as the role model in the region. Starting in October 2021, the UAE hosted Expo 2020 Dubai (delayed because of Covid), where over 190 countries exhibited their achievements to the world. Several NGOs and some major Western international organizations called for a boycott because of UAE human rights abuses. The UAE is not perfect—no country is—but I believe it is a mistake not to endorse what the UAE has done well just because it is not perfect. The world pays attention to what the United States says, and when it does not give an unqualified endorsement to the UAE and its progress and success, other countries in the region that are far less perfect look around and decide it is not worthwhile to strive for the UAE's level of success. The UAE believes that its success has been enabled by its pursuit of greater inclusivity and protection of human rights.

Among nations of the Islamic world, the UAE represents modernity and coexistence, as do Bahrain and Morocco. Today there is a competition for what Islam will look like around the globe. Will it look like Iran and Afghanistan, or like the UAE and Bahrain? The United States has enormous sway in which model of Islam will be most influential on more than a billion people. The Trump administration was unabashedly in favor of supporting and promoting the sphere of modernity and coexistence, represented by the UAE, Bahrain, and Morocco. The Biden administration has not decisively followed through on the Trump administration's policies here, and the momentum toward regional peace has slowed down.

For the United States to regain the mantle of leadership in the Abraham Accords and restore momentum, far more proactive steps need to be taken. Congress has done its part by inaugurating an Abraham Accords Caucus, whose members are dedicated to using legislative tools to advance and expand the Accords. The administration would do well to invite the leaders of the Accords countries to the White House for a summit to discuss their successes, challenges, and ways to move forward. The president could welcome the countries' ambassadors to the next State of the Union Address and acknowledge them as the peacemakers they are. The Abraham Fund should be restarted and creative means employed to strengthen economic ties between the Accords nations. The world will be watching to see if decisive action is taken to expand the circle of peace in the Middle East.

The elephant in the room is the Islamic Republic of Iran, the source of many if not most of the problems in the Middle East. Whether it is through Hezbollah in Lebanon and Syria, Palestinian Islamic Jihad in Gaza, or the Houthis in Yemen, Iran is a destabilizing force. The Islamic Republic of Iran is an evil enterprise seeking to become an empire. It is on the verge of acquiring nuclear capability and does not conceal its malign intent. The Iranian people deserve better and the region needs better. The Trump administration used every tool in its arsenal to restrict Iran's ability to expand its nefarious activities. These tools included supporting and working closely with our allies in the region, but most important was being very clear in our posture toward Iran.

The current administration's approach to Iran, particularly its willingness to reenter the nuclear deal, requires every country in the region to recalibrate its foreign policy. Some will negotiate their own preemptive surrender, some will work to deter and delay Iran's development of a nuclear program, and others will take a wait-and-see approach. The single best measure that the United States can take to support the Abraham Accords and safeguard the region is to be crystal clear on Iran. We must have bright red lines and be prepared to enforce them. Preventing Iran from escalating its malicious actions and from getting nuclear weapons should be a nonpartisan ideal.

38

EMBRACING
EXCEPTIONALISM

―――――――――――――

How should we approach our foreign policy going forward? The first fundamental key for a successful Middle East policy is: Do what is best for your country. Otherwise, no one will respect you, and without respect in the Middle East, you are weak, and if you are weak, people die. The corollary is to expect your friends and allies to act in their own interest. Our job is to create the best conditions for the success of our allies, and build incentives for countries who are not yet our allies to strive to be allies.

We can try to persuade other countries to act in line with our wishes, and provide incentives to so do, but they will put their own interests first. For example, consider the issue of U.S. competition with China. The Israeli market was excited about the infusion of Chinese investment capital. Many Israeli companies start as tech companies, and before they develop into full-fledged growth companies their technology is purchased and they "exit." For Israeli tech entrepreneurs, the result is the same whether they exit to a Western company or a Chinese company. In fact, the more competition for their technology, the higher the valuation will be. This creates wealth for Israelis, boosts the Israeli economy, and gives Israel greater security. That is good for Israel, and because Israel is our ally, it is good for us. Except that the story does not end there. As noted earlier, the coming decades will be all about technological supremacy. The United States, as Israel's number one ally, has the right to ask Israel to be aware of which technologies it sells to China (or other possible foes), since that technology may come back to bite Israel or its allies, particularly the United States. Israel needs to determine if what the United States is asking for is reasonable or not, and then weigh the risks and the benefits involved in its choices.

Similarly, during the debate over the application of Israeli sovereignty in parts of the West Bank, Israel showed the United States various options it was contemplating, the United States explained how it would react to each, and then Israel made a decision in that light. This itself was an exercise of sovereignty, in the sense of making independent decisions for yourself, by yourself. Like other countries, Israel should take in information and opinions from allies, and also from foes and competitors, but ultimately do what is best for itself. Israel is older than half the countries in the United Nations. It should be charting its own course, its own future, and not looking over its shoulder constantly as to what the U.S. State Department will say.

So the first fundamental key to a successful foreign policy is: Do what is best for America. This is not as complicated as experts want to make it out to be. Second, we should expect other countries to have their own best interest in mind, and then formulate our policies accordingly.

Another key is to make sure the world knows what it takes to be either friend or foe, and what follows from being one or the other. If there are no benefits to being a friend and no consequences to being a foe, diplomacy will be ineffective, as countries making decisions in their own interest will have no incentive to consider American opinion in their calculus. Average Americans are frustrated when the United States spends enormous sums on projects around the world that don't really solve problems, and worse, that don't bring us much appreciation or reciprocity in the ways that other countries can reciprocate, such as support for our policy positions in international bodies like the UN and NATO. When Americans question the point of those costly projects, they are told that they do not understand the bigger picture. Ironically, the emperor indeed has no clothes. It was the people promoting those programs who did not understand the bigger picture.

The Trump administration understood the big picture. It did not always act on it, and when it did act, it wasn't always with as much clarity as it should have demonstrated. But I don't know a single decision that was made in my tenure with the U.S. government that didn't begin and end with the question: How can this decision or action make the United States stronger, safer, and more prosperous? If there was no good answer to that question, the action was not a priority of ours. In that context, why did the president put out the Peace to Prosperity Vision? Because it makes our ally Israel safer, stronger and more secure, and it sends a message to other countries about consequences and rewards. It also let the Palestinians know specifically what they can do to advance their cause, and what practices they must end—such as pay-for-slay—if they want to move forward with the blessing of the United States.

What should we expect of our leaders moving forward, whether they are members of Congress, state leaders, or the president? First, we need to elect leaders who see America as the greatest force for good in history, regardless of political party. Much of the rest of the world sees us that way. It is time that all of our leaders felt the same way. Once our leaders are elected, we need to demand that they make their decisions in the best interest of the United States, not in the best interest of the foreign policy think tank cottage industry.

We should reward our best friends by standing resolutely with them, especially if everyone else is too often against them. The world pays a ridiculously disproportionate amount of attention to the Israeli-Palestinian conflict, in votes at the United Nations, discussion at international conferences, and so on. When the international community speaks out on this issue, it is always against Israel. For example, the Paris Climate Accord addresses the Israeli-Palestinian conflict, and not in a neutral way. You may wonder what in the world that conflict has to do with the climate, when no other international conflict areas are mentioned.

A trade agreement that Israel signed with an Asian country in 2020 does not include Jerusalem, the Golan Heights, or any of the West Bank as part of Israel. These are the same carve-outs that western European countries have in their trade agreements with Israel. This Asian country does not make the Israeli-Palestinian conflict a significant part of its foreign policy, so why did it insist on those carve-outs? It is because those western European countries threatened the Asian country with adverse effects to their own trade agreements with that country. It takes a special type of hostility to condition your trade with another country upon how it defines and trades with Israel. Show me any other democratic country in the world that triggers this kind of reaction from any other country. There is none.

You can call it anti-Semitism—it probably is—or you can call it simply an entrenched system protecting itself. Decades ago, some foreign policy experts decided that depriving Israel of defensible borders and a capital city of Jerusalem were bedrock policies, and these notions took on the air of sacred truth. They were embedded into the system until President Trump and his team looked at them and decided they didn't further the interests of the United States, so we were going to change course. The Trump policies clearly worked, but if their benefit is to be permanent, they need to become U.S. policy going forward.

I find ambivalence on the question of standing with Israel more abhorrent than blatant anti-Semitism. Recently, Vice President Harris was speaking at George Mason University when a student asked how the United States can stand by Israel as it practices ethnic genocide. The vice president responded with something along the lines of: You are entitled to your truths, and those truths are very painful. To me, this was shameful leadership by our vice president. She stood in a university classroom in the United States of America and nodded along while a student accused our democratic ally of committing genocide, and then followed up with an ambiguous answer that did not challenge the student's accusation. If our vice president won't stand up to blatant anti-Semitic lies in a classroom in the United States, how could we expect any moral clarity from this administration at the United Nations or at the International Criminal Court?

On the basis of virulent academic myths about alleged Israeli war crimes and so-called apartheid, questioning Israel's right to exist has increasingly been considered a valid intellectual exercise for elite scholars and influential pundits. Someone who would be disinvited from a fancy party for being racist or sexist might be given the head table and plenty of attention for openly questioning whether Israel has a right to exist. This theme has become not only an accepted part of academic discourse, but a dominant and respected view on elite campuses and throughout Europe. Bias against Israel goes hand in hand with a broader hostility toward Jews, whether as cause or effect. While our society has progressed to the point where it is rightly considered totally unacceptable to call someone the n-word or a "kike," anti-Semitism is becoming more prevalent in both elite and popular culture.

Perhaps the most glaring example is Congresswoman Ilhan Omar's unending train of anti-Israel and anti-Semitic comments. Congress, which is currently controlled by her colleagues in the Democratic Party, will only censure discrimination generically, in a kind of dodge, and not anti-Semitism as a specific danger. If no one stands consistently and adamantly against anti-Semitism, it isn't the Jewish people who will be the biggest losers, it will be America. When America shrinks from moral responsibility and leadership, America has lost its way. That is what Ambassador Friedman told me in our first conversation after I said I was unqualified to work for him as an observant Jew. He was determined to confront the nefarious moral relativism that indulges hatred of Jews where other forms of discrimination would be condemned. When it is acceptable to attack Israel using methods, ideas, and language that would immediately be confronted if they targeted any other nation or people, the floodgates for moral relativism open up.

Israel is the proverbial canary in the coal mine. What becomes permissible to do to Israel will ultimately be considered permissible to do to the rest of the West. Challenges to policies have mutated into attacks on the country's foundations. Israel was the world's darling for a brief period of time, from its founding as a state in 1948 until the Six-Day War in 1967. Then voices on what was considered the fringe began accusing Israel of apartheid and various human rights violations. Terrorists were glorified as freedom fighters. A narrative questioning Israel's right to exist began to creep from the fringe to the mainstream of progressive thought. What started with academics questioning Israel's policies has now produced a climate where it is less safe than at any time in the past fifty years for Jews to wear Israeli or Jewish paraphernalia on the streets of New York, Los Angeles, Paris, or London.

I believe that the increasing acceptance of anti-Israel sentiment and outright anti-Semitism is directly connected with the rise of the "progressive" agenda. Consider that the Women's March, Black Lives Matter, and the Dyke March all have the liberation of Palestine and the destruction of Israel as a component of their mission statements. What in the world does Israel or the Palestinians have to do with any of these movements? The answer is the concept of equity, in which the successful must be pulled down if the stragglers cannot be sufficiently lifted up. Advancing the equity agenda is a surefire way to degrade and damage Israel, because it means that Israel is treated unfairly while Palestinian terrorists are indulged.

In America, we first saw one person taking a knee during the national anthem, one academic conference dedicated to the evil of the founding of America, one riot called a "mostly peaceful" protest. We are now seeing assaults on the foundations of America, with Critical Race Theory, the *New York Times*'s 1619 Project, endless ridicule of the Founding Fathers and their principles, and attacks on organized religion. Statues are attacked as though they were living enemies, and names of institutions are changed because of flaws in the character of the person for whom they were named. We have witnessed a systematic attempt to uproot our history and paint America as an inherently flawed country steeped in racism and other forms of bigotry. We have seen rioting across the land. The foundations of our country seem far shakier than just a decade ago.

America succeeds when it embraces its exceptionalism. It excels when it knows and believes it is the greatest force for good in the history of the world. America wins at home and abroad when it channels the blessings of America into the responsibility of leadership. One way that leadership is seen on the world stage is in standing with friends, and over the four years that I was at the U.S. Embassy in Israel the world saw America's unapologetic leadership manifested in our greatly enhanced relationship with Israel.

39

TWO FLAGS

During my first two years at the embassy, I explained the meaning of the Israeli flag to nearly every group I spoke with in Israel. From the time of the first efforts to establish an independent Jewish state in Palestine when it was under Roman rule, two thousand years passed before the Nation of Israel gained sovereignty in its biblical homeland. A great deal of thought was given to Israel's national symbols. There are not many symbols in Judaism, so the design of the flag was taken directly from the prayer shawl, or tallit. The prayer shawl itself derives from a commandment in the book of Numbers, which says it must be adorned with royal blue.

Nahmanadies, a biblical commentator from the eleventh century, pondered why the color blue is specified. He explained that when you see the blue on the prayer shawl, you will be reminded of the blueness of the ocean. Then you will also be reminded of the blueness of the sky. In turn, you will be reminded that the thrown of glory upon which God himself sits is royal blue. The color blue on the shawl therefore reminds you that "we answer to a higher authority," as the Hebrew National hotdog company's slogan puts it, and this understanding will guide you to the correct course of action. I believe that the horizontal stripes in the flag remind us of the sky above and the ocean below.

Now you might ask: If we know that the throne of glory is blue, why not go straight to it without first going through the ocean and the sky? After all, Israel is where the Waze technology was created, to help you navigate from point A to point B in the most efficient way. Here is the answer I share with the groups who come to visit: If you take a cup of water from the ocean, it is clear, not blue. When do you see the blueness of the ocean? Only when you see all the cups of water in the ocean together. If you could take a cup of air from the sky, it too would be clear. When do you see the blueness of the sky? Only when you see all the cups in the air together. Thinking about the ocean and the sky teaches us an important lesson: Every cup of water matters. Every cup of air matters.

When you answer to a higher authority, you must have perspective and humility, and understand that you need partners to fulfill a higher purpose. The flag of Israel is a symbol not of perfection, but of a dream, a vision, of something worth sacrificing for. It teaches about the need for humility and perspective, and it reminds us that every effort big and small has the potential to matter a great deal.

In Israel, I learned how much Israelis respect their flag. I learned that they also respect the American flag. When respect for the national flag is up for debate in our country, we have some serious soul-searching to do as a nation.

In February 2017, I was offered a position to be the senior advisor to Ambassador David Friedman at our embassy in Jerusalem. I was given two diplomatic passports because the State Department did not imagine it would be possible for me to use the same passport to go to Israel and then to other countries in the region. On January 20, 2021, at 7 p.m. Israel time, my letter of resignation took effect. I resigned as Ambassador Friedman's senior advisor, his chief of staff of the U.S. Embassy in Jerusalem. I also resigned as the special envoy for economic normalization and the director of the Abraham Fund. I turned in both diplomatic passports, and I am pleased that although I traveled to many Arab and Muslim countries, I never used my second passport. I never needed to, nor should anyone else in the future. The only item I didn't turn in was my U.S. flag lapel pin. I wear it every day, and while I don't represent the United States of America in any official capacity today, just having the flag on my lapel reminds me that I have received one of the greatest blessings in history, and that is to be an American. And because I have received this blessing, it comes with responsibility, I matter, and I have purpose and a mission. This mission is not merely to maintain America for the next generation, but to help make America even greater for the next generation.

To the team that takes on the banner of the Abraham Accords in this or any future administration, the symbolism of the U.S. flag should be your guide. If you follow the message of the flag and honor the greatness of the United States of America, you will recognize the merit of bringing more willing countries into the Abraham Accords. If that happens, the Middle East will be changed for the better in our lifetime. These are words I could not have imagined saying when David Friedman offered me a position during that train ride from Washington, D.C., back to New York. I expected to learn a lot more about Israel and its neighbors in my job, and I did. But what really changed me is that I came to understood the true power and greatness of the United States of America.

God bless the Abraham Accords, God bless our allies, and God bless America.

ACKNOWLEDGMENTS

I really enjoy giving speeches and interactive talks. While I was working at the U.S. Embassy in Israel, one of my favorite activities was meeting with groups of people and telling the story of the U.S.-Israel relationship and why it is important to America. It was truly a labor of love for me, and pre-Covid it was not unusual for me to speak with two or three groups a day, in addition to my core responsibilities as chief of staff to the most consequential U.S. ambassador to Israel in history. In total, I spoke to thousands of people. As much as I enjoy speaking, I dislike writing. It is simply a labor. Yet I wrote this book because I do not currently have a platform to speak to hundreds of groups a year. The purpose of this book is to let my people, the American people, know why the U.S.-Israel relationship is so important.

I would not have written this book without the insistence of Jonathan Bronitsky from Athos, who was very encouraging through the entire process. I have now become friends too with Carol, Amanda, and Sam at Encounter Books. Without their assistance, this book would not be as organized or well written as it is. I greatly appreciate their help in sharpening my ideas so they will live on.

As for my embassy job, I owed that to David Friedman, and this book demonstrates why it was an honor to work for him. He was more than a boss; he became a close friend. Tammy Friedman treated my family like her own, and we are forever in her debt. There were so many people at the embassy who worked tirelessly in challenging circumstances, and our relationships became stronger for it. I am grateful for the efforts of Mati, Russ, Gene, Cynthia, Curtis, Michael, Jen, and so many more. Special appreciation goes to our military attachés, who exemplified mission without politics. Thanks to Jonathan Shrier, who as deputy chief of mission helped manage the embassy during the days of Covid and the Abraham Accords. The front office staff and I worked incredibly closely as a team, so thank you to Drew, Lisa, Therese, and of course Sandy!

The embassy is its own community and everyone from the marines to the ambassador to the phone operators and the foreign service officers plays an important role in its success. There are too many to name, but I want to thank all, from the security teams to the drivers to the people who cared for our homes and those who worked the mail room: You made my family's adjustment to embassy life easier and for that I am grateful.

A big thank you goes to David Milstein, who always pushed the team to accomplish more.

Among the White House team that I worked closely with over four years, I especially want to recognize Thomas Storch, Miguel Correa, John Rader, Rob Greenway, Eddie Vazquez, Ryan Arant, and Scott Leith. I learned much from them and had great fun too.

Thank you to President Trump for your leadership. You were the greatest president for the U.S.-Israel relationship in history.

Jared Kushner had an extraordinarily consequential position and filled it with vision, humility, and great success. Thank you to Jared and his entire team, led by Avi Berkowitz, Cassidy Luna, and Charlton Boyd.

Thank you to Vice President Pence, Secretary Pompeo, Secretary Mnuchin, Secretary Brouillette, and Ambassador Haley. It is unlikely that in any other administration a chief of staff at an embassy in Israel would have gotten to work closely with you and your teams. I was a great beneficiary of your leadership and friendship.

Many people in D.C. helped to keep Israel front and center and to keep all the players in sync. For that I thank my friends and colleagues Jon Lerner, Mitch Silk, Eli Miller, Victoria Coates, Ezra Cohen, and many more.

I could not have been successful at work if not for the people who helped my wife and kids transition to life in Israel with ease and grace. To the entire Raanana community, especially those who went above and beyond, I am grateful.

In my embassy position I had the opportunity to meet with titans of industry in the United States and Israel. I am honored to consider them friends and colleagues. Thank you to Miriam, Safra, Gal, Marius, Yossi, Yariv, Michael, Elie, Eli, Yair, David, Ovi, Scott, Joseph, and many others who personify the strength of the U.S.-Israel relationship.

It was an honor working with my counterparts in the Israeli government and in the Abraham Accords countries. Thank you to Yoav, Yonatan, Ronen, Lior, Edna, Orit, Asher, Maoz, Itai, Shiri, Tariq, Abdulla, Yousef, and many more. I am forever appreciative of your professionalism and friendship.

My job wasn't easy, though I tried not to complain to many people because I knew that many would have been thrilled to have my position. But when I needed a sympathetic ear, I was blessed to have friends like Paul Packer, Eric Herschmann, Baruch Glaubach, and Ushi Shafran.

My parents raised their children to try to make a difference in the world. When this opportunity came up for me, the timing wasn't perfect but the opportunity was. Thank you, Mom and Dad, for teaching us to grab the opportunity to make a difference whenever we can. Thank you to my in-laws, Danny and Carol, for instilling the same values in my wife, Estee.

My kids—Akiva, Shayna, Simcha, and Atara—didn't get the father they deserved during the four years I worked at the embassy. I wrote this book in part to show them what their sacrifice of my attention was for. It is as much their history as mine. Finally, there are not enough words to express my appreciation and love for my incredible wife, Estee. For four years she wrote a blog describing ordinary people with an extraordinary opportunity. Estee, you have made sure that we remember that we are ordinary but capable of extraordinary things. Thank you for all of the love, support, and partnership. This adventure was not mine, it was ours, and you are the one who ensured it would be an adventure for our kids as well.

INDEX